"This is the book to hand anyone who has been inquiring about or struggling with the tenets of Calvinism in general, and with the subject of election in particular. It is easily read, finely illustrated, and belongs in the library of every Christian. I recommend it highly."

JAY E. ADAMS, general editor of The Journal of Modern Ministry

"Chosen by God by R. C. Sproul is a classic of twentieth century Reformed literature. Nothing has surpassed it in clarity or passion. Those who count this volume as 'life-changing' are legion. I am ecstatic that it has been made available for a new generation to discover."

DEREK W. H. THOMAS, John E. Richards professor of systematic and practical theology, Reformed Theological Seminary–Jackson; minister of teaching, First Presbyterian Church in Jackson, Mississippi; editorial director of Alliance of Confessing Evangelicals

"In simple, succinct, and scriptural terms, this little book is packed with big implications about how God saves."

MARK DRISCOLL, pastor of Mars Hill Church; president of Acts 29 and The Resurgence

"R. C. Sproul has long ago established his position as one of the most effective communicators of the great truths of Reformed theology. Chosen by God is an outstandingly helpful treatment of the doctrine of predestination. Characteristically, it is clear in both thought and expression, consistently led by Biblical teaching, and yet very lively in style and highly readable."

ERIC J. ALEXANDER, retired senior minister of St. George's Tron Church in Glasgow, Scotland

"Christians belong to God because we have been chosen by him. This simple truth is little understood by people who have been led to imagine that it is they who have chosen God and not the other way around. Dr. Sproul has shown us with the clarity that is his hallmark just what this means for us and why it is so important."

DR. GERALD BRAY, research professor of divinity, Beeson Divinity School, Samford University; author of Holiness and the Will of God

"Every generation is under a biblical mandate to provide a legacy for the coming generation that honors the Lord and propels them with insight and encouragement rooted in the glorious Gospel of our Savior, Jesus Christ. Dr. R. C. Sproul in the Holiness of God *and* Chosen by God *has provided such a legacy for the next generation. One generation stacks up stones to the praise of God to teach the next generation. Here are two stones from the stack that give praise to God! Open these books and you will find the biblical truth insightfully illustrated and challengingly communicated. May the Lord do great things through you as you profit from these works until he comes in glory."*

DR. HARRY REEDER III, senior minister of Briarwood Presbyterian in Birmingham, Alabama

"With characteristic clarity and charity, Chosen by God *gives us biblical wisdom on an issue that has for centuries vexed the church—how are we to understand God's sovereign power and man's responsibility? The book has helped tens of thousands of Christians not only find answers, but find peace."*

DR. R. C. SPROUL JR., founder of Highlands Ministries; teaching fellow, Ligonier Ministries

CHOSEN BY GOD

Chosen
by God

R. C. SPROUL

TYNDALE HOUSE PUBLISHERS, INC.
CAROL STREAM, ILLINOIS

Visit Tyndale's exciting Web site at www.tyndale.com.

TYNDALE and Tyndale's quill logo are registered trademarks of Tyndale House Publishers, Inc.

Chosen by God

Library of Congress Catalog Card Number 86-50651

ISBN 978-0-8423-0282-1 (hc)
ISBN 978-0-8423-1335-3 (sc)
ISBN 978-0-8423-7212-1 (mass)

Printed in the United States of America

16 15 14 13
22 21 20 19 18

CONTENTS

PREFACE

It has now been a quarter of a century since I first penned *Chosen by God*, and in the ensuing years, I've had several surprises about this work. When I first wrote it, I had the sense that I was "writing to the choir." That is, I doubted very much whether people who were not already convinced of the Reformed doctrine of election would trouble themselves by reading this particular work. And so I thought, *It's worth my time to write it if only for the benefit of those who already are convinced of the doctrine and who need a little deeper understanding of election and how to articulate it to others.*

As things turned out, I have been astonished by the response of the general public to this book. Literally thousands of people have indicated to me either personally or by letter that it has served to change their thinking and convince them that the Reformed view of election is indeed the biblical view. They've come to agree with Spurgeon's sentiment that Reformed theology is only a nickname for biblical Christianity. But not everyone who's read this book has been persuaded by its posture.

I've also had another surprise with respect to some who have read it and another book of mine called *The Holiness of God*. Of all of the books that I've published, it has had the widest distribution. What I have heard frequently from people who read both *The Holiness of God* and *Chosen by God* is this. They tell me that reading *The Holiness of God* changed their lives by giving them an epiphany of the majesty and grandeur of our God. They say they loved that book and the awakening that they experienced in reading it, yet at the same time, they found *Chosen by God* somewhat distasteful in comparison. When people tell me that, I usually respond by saying, "I think that either you didn't understand what I was saying in *The Holiness of God* or you haven't understood what I say in *Chosen by God*." God's holiness encompasses his sovereignty, and we cannot drive a wedge between the two. We may distinguish them but never separate them.

My hope, for those of you who are reading this book for the first time or those who are rereading it in its updated version, is that you will come not only to be persuaded of the truth of the doctrine of election as expounded by the Reformers, but that you will see the sweetness of it and come to love it and see how it opens wide to our understanding the whole dimension of the grace and mercy of God. Martin Luther said to Erasmus in the 16th century that if you don't embrace *sola gratia*, that is salvation by grace alone, you haven't comprehended *sola fide*, justification by faith alone. The two are twin towers of the Biblical understanding of salvation—*sola fide* and *sola gratia*, which together drive us to the final sola—*Soli Deo Gloria*.

R. C. Sproul

Holy Week, 2010

Acknowledgments

I continue to be extremely grateful for the work that Tyndale House Publishers has done in the original compilation of this book and the distribution of it and the care that they have given to this whole project.

CHAPTER ONE

THE STRUGGLE

B aseball. Hot dogs. Apple pie. Chevrolet. These are all things American. To complete the mix we must add the great American motto: "We will not discuss religion or politics."

Mottoes are made to be broken. Perhaps no American rule is broken more frequently than the one about not discussing religion or politics. We embark on such discussions repeatedly. And when the topic turns to religion it sometimes gravitates to the issue of predestination. Sadly, that often means the end of discussion and the beginning of argument, yielding more heat than light.

Arguing about predestination is virtually irresistible. (Pardon the pun.) The topic is so juicy. It provides an opportunity to spar about all things philosophical. When the issue flares up we suddenly become super-patriotic, guarding the tree of human liberty with more zeal and tenacity than Patrick Henry ever dreamed of. The specter of an all-powerful God making choices for us, and perhaps even against us, makes us scream, "Give me free will or give me death!"

The very word *predestination* has an ominous ring to it. It is linked to the despairing notion of fatalism and somehow suggests that within its pale we are reduced to meaningless puppets. The word conjures up visions of a diabolical deity who plays capricious games with our lives. We seem to be subjected to the whims of horrible decrees that were fixed in concrete long before we were born. Better that our lives were fixed by the stars, for then at least we could find clues to our destiny in the daily horoscopes.

Add to the horror of the word *predestination* the public image of its most famous teacher, John Calvin, and we shudder all the more. We see Calvin portrayed as a stern and grim-faced tyrant, a sixteenth-century Ichabod Crane who found fiendish delight in the burning of recalcitrant heretics. It is enough to cause us to retreat from the discussion altogether and reaffirm our commitment never to discuss religion and politics.

With a topic people find so unpleasant, it is a wonder that we ever discuss it at all. Why do we speak of it? Because we enjoy unpleasantness? Not at all. We discuss it because we cannot avoid it. It is a doctrine plainly set forth in the Bible. We talk about predestination because the Bible talks about predestination. If we desire to build our theology on the Bible, we run head on into this concept. We soon discover that John Calvin did not invent it.

Virtually all Christian churches have some formal doctrine of predestination. To be sure, the doctrine of predestination found in the Roman Catholic Church is different from that in the Presbyterian Church. The Lutherans have a different view of the matter from the Methodists.

The fact that such variant views of predestination abound only underscores the fact that if we are biblical in our thinking we must have some doctrine of predestination. We cannot ignore such well-known passages as:

> Just as He chose us in Him before the foundation of the
> world, that we should be holy and without blame before
> Him in love, having predestined us to adoption as sons by

Jesus Christ to Himself, according to the good pleasure of His will . . . (Ephesians 1:4-5)

In whom also we have obtained an inheritance, being predestined according to the purpose of Him who works all things according to the counsel of His will . . . (Ephesians 1:11)

For whom He foreknew, He also predestined to be conformed to the image of His Son, that He might be the firstborn among many brethren. (Romans 8:29)

If we are to be biblical, then, the issue is not whether we should have a doctrine of predestination or not, but what kind we should embrace. If the Bible is the Word of God, not mere human speculation, and if God himself declares that there is such a thing as predestination, then it follows irresistibly that we must embrace some doctrine of predestination.

If we are to follow this line of thinking, then, of course, we must go one step further. It is not enough to have just any view of predestination. It is our duty to seek the correct view of predestination, lest we be guilty of distorting or ignoring the Word of God. Here is where the real struggle begins, the struggle to sort out accurately all that the Bible teaches about this matter.

My struggle with predestination began early in my Christian life. I knew a professor of philosophy in college who was a convinced Calvinist. He set forth the so-called "Reformed" view of predestination. I did not like it. I did not like it at all. I fought against it tooth and nail all the way through college.

I graduated from college unconvinced of the Reformed or Calvinistic view of predestination only to go to a seminary that included on its staff the king of the Calvinists, John H. Gerstner.

Gerstner is to predestination what Einstein is to physics or what Tiger Woods is to golf. I would rather have challenged Einstein on relativity or entered into match play with Woods than to take on Gerstner. But . . . fools rush in where angels fear to tread.

I challenged Gerstner in the classroom time after time, making a total pest of myself. I resisted for well over a year. My final surrender came in stages. Painful stages. It started when I began work as a student pastor in a church. I wrote a note to myself that I kept on my desk in a place where I could always see it.

YOU ARE REQUIRED TO BELIEVE, TO PREACH, AND TO TEACH WHAT THE BIBLE SAYS IS TRUE, NOT WHAT YOU WANT THE BIBLE TO SAY IS TRUE.

The note haunted me. My final crisis came in my senior year. I had a three-credit course in the study of Jonathan Edwards. We spent the semester studying Edwards's most famous book, *The Freedom of the Will*, under Gerstner's tutelage. At the same time I had a Greek exegesis course in the book of Romans. I was the only student in that course, one on one with the New Testament professor. There was nowhere I could hide.

The combination was too much for me. Gerstner, Edwards, the New Testament professor, and above all the apostle Paul, were too formidable a team for me to withstand. The ninth chapter of Romans was the clincher. I simply could find no way to avoid the apostle's teaching in that chapter. Reluctantly, I sighed and surrendered, but with my head, not my heart. "OK, I believe this stuff, but I don't have to like it!"

I soon discovered that God has created us so that the heart is supposed to follow the head. I could not, with impunity, love something with my head that I hated in my heart. Once I began to see the cogency of the doctrine and its broader implications, my eyes were opened to the graciousness of grace and to the grand comfort of God's sovereignty. I began to like the doctrine little by little, until it burst upon my soul that the doctrine revealed the depth and the riches of the mercy of God.

I no longer feared the demons of fatalism or the ugly thought that I was being reduced to a puppet. Now I rejoiced in a gracious Savior who alone was immortal, invisible, the only wise God.

They say there is nothing more obnoxious than a converted drunk. Try a converted Arminian. Converted Arminians tend to become flaming Calvinists, zealots for the cause of predestination. You are reading the work of such a convert.

My struggle has taught me a few things along the way. I have learned, for example, that not all Christians are as zealous about predestination as I am. There are better men than I who do not share my conclusions. I have learned that many misunderstand predestination. I have also learned the pain of being wrong.

When I teach the doctrine of predestination I am often frustrated by those who obstinately refuse to submit to it. I want to scream, "Don't you realize you are resisting the Word of God?" In these cases I am guilty of at least one of two possible sins. If my understanding of predestination is correct, then at best I am being impatient with people who are merely struggling as I once did, and at worst I am being arrogant and patronizing toward those who disagree with me.

If my understanding of predestination is not correct, then my sin is compounded, since I would be slandering the saints who by opposing my view are fighting for the angels. So the stakes are high for me in this matter.

The struggle about predestination is all the more confusing because the greatest minds in the history of the church have disagreed about it. Scholars and Christian leaders, past and present, have taken different stands. A brief glance at church history reveals that the debate over predestination is not between liberals and conservatives or between believers and unbelievers. It is a debate among believers, among godly and earnest Christians.

It may be helpful to see how the great teachers of the past line up on the question.

"Reformed" view	*Opposing views*
Augustine	Pelagius
Thomas Aquinas	Jacob Arminius
Martin Luther	Philip Melanchthon
John Calvin	John Wesley
Jonathan Edwards	Charles Finney

It must look like I am trying to stack the deck. Those thinkers who are most widely regarded as the titans of classical Christian scholarship fall heavily on the Reformed side. I am persuaded, however, that this is a fact of history that dare not be ignored. To be sure, it is possible that Augustine, Aquinas, Luther, Calvin, and Edwards could all be wrong on this matter. These men certainly disagree with each other on other points of doctrine. They are neither individually nor collectively infallible.

We cannot determine truth by counting noses. The great thinkers of the past can be wrong. But it is important for us to see that the Reformed doctrine of predestination was not invented by John Calvin. There is nothing in Calvin's view of predestination that was not earlier propounded by Luther and Augustine before him. Later, Lutheranism did not follow Luther on this matter but Melanchthon, who altered his views after Luther's death. It is also noteworthy that in his famous treatise on theology, *Institutes of the Christian Religion*, John Calvin wrote sparingly on the subject. Luther wrote more about predestination than did Calvin.

The history lesson aside, we must take seriously the fact that such learned men agreed on this difficult subject. Again, that they agreed does not prove the case for predestination. They could have been wrong. But it gets our attention. We cannot dismiss the Reformed view as a peculiarly Presbyterian notion. I know that during my great struggle with predestination I was deeply troubled by the unified voices of the titans of classical Christian scholarship on this point. Again, they are not infallible, but they deserve our respect and an honest hearing.

Among contemporary Christian leaders we find a more balanced list of agreement and disagreement. (Keep in mind that we are speaking here in general terms and that there are significant points of difference among those on each side.)

"Reformed" view	*Opposing views*
Sinclair Ferguson	C. S. Lewis
Michael Horton	Roger Olson
John MacArthur	Grant Osborne
John Piper	Clark Pinnock
Francis Schaeffer	Billy Graham

I don't know where Chuck Swindoll, Pat Robertson, and a lot of other leaders stand on this point. Jimmy Swaggart has made it clear that he considers the Reformed view a demonic heresy. His attacks on the doctrine have been less than sober. They do not reflect the care and earnestness of the men listed above in the "opposing" column. They are all great leaders whose views are worthy of our close attention.

My hope is that we will all continue to struggle with the truth. We must never assume that we have arrived. Yet there is no virtue in sheer skepticism. We look with a jaundiced eye at those who are always learning but never coming to a knowledge of the truth. God is delighted with men and women of conviction. Of course he is concerned that our convictions be according to truth. Struggle with me, then, as we embark upon the difficult but, I hope, profitable journey examining the doctrine of predestination.

For Further Study

> The king's heart is in the hand of the LORD, Like the rivers of water; He turns it wherever He wishes. (PROVERBS 21:1)

> For truly against Your holy Servant Jesus, whom You anointed, both Herod and Pontius Pilate, with the Gentiles and the people of Israel, were gathered together to do whatever Your hand and Your purpose determined before to be done. (ACTS 4:27-28)

> And we know that all things work together for good to those who love God, to those who are the called according to His purpose. For whom He foreknew, He also predestined to be conformed to the image of His Son, that He might be the firstborn among many brethren. Moreover whom He predestined, these He also called; whom He called, these He also justified; and whom He justified, these He also glorified. (ROMANS 8:28-30)

*Blessed be the God and Father of our Lord Jesus Christ, who has
blessed us with every spiritual blessing in the heavenly places
in Christ, just as He chose us in Him before the foundation of
the world, that we should be holy and without blame before
Him in love, having predestined us to adoption as sons by
Jesus Christ to Himself, according to the good pleasure of His
will, to the praise of the glory of His grace, by which He made
us accepted in the Beloved.* (EPHESIANS 1:3-6)

CHAPTER TWO

PREDESTINATION AND THE SOVEREIGNTY OF GOD

As we struggle through the doctrine of predestination, we must start with a clear understanding of what the word means. Here we encounter difficulties immediately. Our definition is often colored by our doctrine. We might hope that if we turn to a neutral source for our definition—a source like Webster's dictionary—we will escape such prejudice. No such luck. (Or should I say, no such providence.) Look at these entries in *Webster's New Collegiate Dictionary*.

predestinate: *destined, fated, or determined beforehand; to foreordain to an earthly or eternal lot or destiny by divine decree.*

predestination: *the doctrine that God in consequence of his foreknowledge of all events infallibly guides those who are destined for salvation.*

predestine: *to destine, decree, determine, appoint, or settle beforehand.*

I am not sure how much we can learn from these dictionary definitions other than that Noah Webster must have been a Lutheran. What we can glean, however, is that predestination has something to do with the relationship of our ultimate destination and that something is done about that destination by somebody before we arrive there. The *pre-* of predestination refers to time. Webster speaks of "beforehand." Destiny refers to the place we are going, as we see in the normal use of the word *destination*.

When I call my travel agent to book a flight, the question is soon raised: "What is your destination?" Sometimes the question is put more simply: "Where are you going?" Our destination is the place where we are going. In theology it refers to one of two places; either we are going to heaven or we are going to hell. In either case, we cannot cancel the trip. God gives us but two final options. One or the other is our final destination. Even Roman Catholicism, which has another place beyond the grave, purgatory, views that as an intermediate stop along the way. Their travelers ride the local while Protestants prefer the express route.

What predestination means, in its most elementary form, is that our final destination, heaven or hell, is decided by God not only before we get there, but before we are even born. It teaches that our ultimate destiny is in the hands of God. Another way of saying it is this: From all eternity, before we existed, God decided to save some members of the human race and to let the rest of the human race perish. God made a choice—he chose some individuals to be saved unto everlasting blessedness in heaven and others he chose to pass over, to allow them to follow the consequences of their sins into eternal torment in hell.

This is a hard saying, no matter how we approach it. We wonder, "Do our individual lives have any bearing on God's decision?

Even though God makes his choice before we are born, he still knows everything about our lives before we live them. Does he take that prior knowledge of us into account when he makes his decision?" How we answer that last question will determine whether our view of predestination is Reformed or not. Remember, we stated earlier that virtually all churches have *some* doctrine of predestination. Most churches agree that God's decision is made before we are born. The issue then rests upon the question, "On what basis does God make that decision?"

Before we set out to answer that, we must clarify one other point. Frequently, people think about predestination with respect to everyday questions about traffic accidents and the like. They wonder whether God decreed that the Yankees win the World Series or whether the tree fell on their car by divine edict. Even insurance contracts have clauses that refer to "acts of God."

Questions such as these are normally treated in theology under the broader heading of Providence. Our study focuses on predestination in the narrow sense, restricting it to the ultimate question of predestined salvation or damnation, what we call *election* and *reprobation*. The other questions are both interesting and important, but they fall beyond the scope of this book.

The Sovereignty of God

In most discussions about predestination, there is great concern about protecting the dignity and freedom of man. But we must also observe the crucial importance of the sovereignty of God. Though God is not a creature, he is personal, with supreme dignity and supreme freedom. We are aware of the ticklish problems surrounding the relationship between God's sovereignty and human freedom. We must also be aware of the close relationship between God's sovereignty and God's freedom. The freedom of a sovereign is always greater than the freedom of his subjects.

When we speak of divine sovereignty we are speaking about God's authority and about God's power. As sovereign, God is the supreme authority of heaven and earth. All other authority is lesser authority. Any other authority that exists in the universe is derived from and dependent upon God's authority. All other forms of authority exist either by God's command or by God's permission.

The word *authority* contains within itself the word *author*. God is the author of all things over which he has authority. He created the universe. He owns the universe. His ownership gives him certain rights. He may do with his universe what is pleasing to his holy will.

Likewise, all power in the universe flows from the power of God. All power in this universe is subordinate to him. Even Satan is powerless without God's sovereign permission to act.

Christianity is not dualism. We do not believe in two ultimate equal powers locked in an eternal struggle for supremacy. If Satan were equal to God, we would have no confidence, no hope of good triumphing over evil. We would be destined to an eternal standoff between two equal and opposing forces.

Satan is a creature. He is evil to be sure, but even his evil is subject to the sovereignty of God, as is our own evil. God's authority is ultimate; his power is omnipotent. He is sovereign.

One of my duties as a seminary professor was to teach the theology of the Westminster Confession of Faith. The Westminster Confession has been the central creedal document for historic Presbyterianism. It sets forth the classical doctrines of the Presbyterian church.

Once, while teaching this course, I announced to my evening

class that the following week we would study the section of the confession dealing with predestination. Since the evening class was open to the public, my students rushed to invite their friends for the juicy discussion. The next week the classroom was packed with students and guests.

I began the class by reading the opening lines from chapter three of the Westminster Confession:

> God, from all eternity, did, by the most wise and holy counsel of His own will, freely, and unchangeably ordain whatsoever comes to pass.

I stopped reading at that point. I asked, "Is there anyone in this room who does not believe the words that I just read?" A multitude of hands went up. I then asked, "Are there any convinced atheists in the room?" No hands were raised. I then said something outrageous: "Everyone who raised his hand to the first question should also have raised his hand to the second question."

A chorus of groans and protests met my statement. How could I accuse someone of atheism for not believing that God foreordains whatever comes to pass? Those who protested these words were not denying the existence of God. They were not protesting against Christianity. They were protesting against Calvinism.

I tried to explain to the class that the idea that God foreordains whatever comes to pass is not an idea unique to Calvinism. It isn't even unique to Christianity. It is simply a tenet of theism—a necessary tenet of theism.

That God in some sense foreordains whatever comes to pass is a necessary result of his sovereignty. In itself it does not plead for Calvinism. It only declares that God is absolutely sovereign over his creation. God can foreordain things in different ways. But everything that happens must at least happen by his permission. If he permits something, then he must decide to allow it. If he decides to allow something, then in a sense he is foreordaining it. Who, among Christians, would argue that God could not stop something in this world from happening? If God so desires, he has the power to stop the whole world.

To say that God foreordains all that comes to pass is simply to say that God is sovereign over his entire creation. If something could come to pass apart from his sovereign permission, then that which came to pass would frustrate his sovereignty. If God refused to permit something to happen and it happened anyway, then whatever caused it to happen would have more authority and power than God himself. If there is any part of creation outside of God's sovereignty, then God is simply not sovereign. If God is not sovereign, then God is not God.

If there is one single molecule in this universe running around loose, totally free of God's sovereignty, then we have no guarantee that a single promise of God will ever be fulfilled. Perhaps that one maverick molecule will lay waste all the grand and glorious plans that God has made and promised to us. If a grain of sand in the kidney of Oliver Cromwell changed the course of English history, so our maverick molecule could change the course of all redemption history. Maybe that one molecule will be the thing that prevents Christ from returning.

We've heard the story: For want of a nail the shoe was lost; for want of the shoe the horse was lost; for want of the horse the rider was lost; for want of the rider the battle was lost; for want of the battle the war was lost. I remember my distress when I heard that Bill Vukovich, the greatest car driver of his era, was killed in a crash in the Indianapolis 500. The cause was later isolated in the failure of a cotter pin that cost ten cents.

Bill Vukovich had amazing control of race cars. He was a magnificent driver. However, he was not sovereign. A part worth only a dime cost him his life. God doesn't have to worry about ten-cent cotter pins wrecking his plans. There are no maverick molecules running around loose. God is sovereign. God is God.

My students began to see that divine sovereignty is not an issue peculiar to Calvinism, or even to Christianity. Without sovereignty God cannot be God. If we reject divine sovereignty then we must embrace atheism. This is the problem we all face. We must hold tightly to God's sovereignty. Yet we must do it in such a way so as not to violate human freedom.

At this point I should do for you what I did for my students in the evening class—finish the statement from the Westminster Confession. The whole statement reads as follows:

> God, from all eternity, did by the most wise and holy counsel of His own will, freely, and unchangeably ordain whatsoever comes to pass: yet so, as thereby neither is God the author of sin, nor is violence offered to the will of the creatures; nor is the liberty or contingency of second causes taken away, but rather established.

Note that, while it affirms God's sovereignty over all things, the Confession also asserts that God does not do evil or violate human freedom. Human freedom and evil are under God's sovereignty.

God's Sovereignty and the Problem of Evil

Surely the most difficult question of all is how evil can coexist with a God who is both altogether holy and altogether sovereign.

I am afraid that most Christians do not realize the profound severity of this problem. Skeptics have called this issue the "Achilles' Heel of Christianity."

I vividly remember the first time I felt the pain of this thorny problem. I was a freshman in college and had been a Christian for only a few weeks. I was playing Ping-Pong in the lounge of the men's dormitory when, in the middle of a volley, the thought struck me: *If God is totally righteous, how could he have created a universe where evil is present? If all things come from God, doesn't evil come from him as well?*

Then, as now, I realized that evil was a problem for the sovereignty of God. Did evil come into the world against God's sovereign will? If so, then he is not absolutely sovereign. If not, then we must conclude that in some sense even evil is foreordained by God.

For years I sought the answer to this problem, scouring the works of theologians and philosophers. I found some clever attempts at resolving the problem but, as yet, have never found a deeply satisfying answer.

The most common solution we hear for this dilemma is a simple reference to man's free will. We hear such statements as, "Evil came into the world by man's free will. Man is the author of sin, not God."

Surely that statement squares with the biblical account of the origin of sin. We know that man was created with a free will and that man freely chose to sin. It was not God who committed sin; it was man. The problem still persists, however. From where did man ever gain the slightest inclination to sin? If he was created with a desire for sin, then a shadow is cast on the integrity of the Creator. If he was created with no desire for sin, then we must ask where that desire came from.

The mystery of sin is tied to our understanding of free will, man's state in creation, and God's sovereignty. The question of free will is so vital to our understanding of predestination that we will devote an entire chapter to the subject. Until then we will restrict our study to the question of man's first sin.

How could Adam and Eve fall? They were created good. We might suggest that their problem was the craftiness of Satan. Satan beguiled them. He tricked them into eating the forbidden fruit. We might suppose that the serpent was so slick that it utterly and completely fooled our original parents.

Such an explanation suffers from several problems. If Adam and Eve did not realize what they were doing, if they were utterly fooled, then the sin would have been all Satan's. But the Bible makes it clear that in spite of his craftiness the serpent spoke directly in challenge to the commandment of God. Adam and Eve had heard God issue his prohibition and warning. They heard Satan contradict God. The decision was squarely before them. They could not appeal to Satan's trickery to excuse them.

Even if Satan not only fooled but forced Adam and Eve to sin, we are still not free of our dilemma. If they could have rightfully said, "The devil made us do it," we would still face the problem of the devil's sin. Where did the devil come from? How did he manage to fall from goodness? Whether we are speaking of the fall of man or the fall of Satan we still are dealing with the problem of good creatures becoming evil.

Again we hear the "easy" explanation that evil came through the creature's free will. Free will is a good thing. That God gave us free will does not cast blame on him. In creation man was given an ability to sin and an ability not to sin. He chose to sin. The question is, "Why?"

Herein lies the problem. Before a person can commit an act of sin he must first have a desire to perform that act. The Bible tells us that evil actions flow from evil desires. But the presence of an evil desire is already sin. We sin because we are sinners. We were born with a sin nature. We are fallen creatures. But Adam and Eve were not created fallen. They had no sin nature. They were good creatures with a free will. Yet they chose to sin. Why? I don't know. Nor have I found anyone yet who does know.

In spite of this excruciating problem we still must affirm that God is not the author of sin. The Bible does not reveal the answers to all our questions. It does reveal the nature and character of God. One thing is absolutely unthinkable, that God could be the author or doer of sin.

But this chapter is about God's sovereignty. We are still left with the question that, given the fact of human sin, how does it relate to God's sovereignty? If it is true that in some sense God foreordains everything that comes to pass, then it follows with no doubt that God must have foreordained the entrance of sin into the world. That is not to say that God forced it to happen or that he imposed evil upon his creation. All that means is that God in his wisdom must have decided to allow it to happen. If he did not allow it to happen, then it could not have happened, or else he is not sovereign.

We know that God is sovereign because we know that God is God. Therefore we must conclude that God foreordained sin. What else can we conclude? We must conclude that God's decision to allow sin to enter the world was a good decision. This is not to say that our sin is really a good thing, but merely that God's allowing us to do sin, which is evil, is a good thing. God's allowing evil is good, but the evil he allows is still evil. God's involvement in all this is perfectly righteous. Our involvement in it is wicked. The fact that God decided to allow us to sin does not absolve us from our responsibility for sin.

A frequent objection we hear is that if God knew in advance that we were going to sin, why did he create us in the first place? One philosopher stated the problem this way: "If God knew we would sin but could not stop it, then he is neither omnipotent nor sovereign. If he could stop it but chose not to, then he is neither loving nor benevolent." By this approach God is made to look bad no matter how we answer the question.

We must assume that God knew in advance that man would fall. We also must assume that he could have intervened to stop it. Or he could have chosen not to create us at all. We grant all those hypothetical possibilities. Bottom line, we know that he knew we would fall and that he went ahead and created us anyway. Why does that mean he is unloving? He also knew in advance that he was going to implement a plan of redemption for his fallen creation that would include a perfect manifestation of his justice and a perfect expression of his love and mercy. It was certainly loving of God to predestine the salvation of his people, those the Bible calls his "elect" or "chosen ones."

It is the non-elect that are the problem. If some people are not elected unto salvation, then it would seem that God is not all that loving toward them. For them it seems that it would have been more loving of God not to have allowed them to be born.

That may indeed be the case. But we must ask the really tough question: Is there any reason that a righteous God ought to be loving toward a creature who hates him and rebels constantly against his divine authority and holiness? The objection raised by the philosopher implies that God owes his love to sinful creatures. That is, the unspoken assumption is that God is obligated to be gracious to sinners. What the philosopher overlooks is that *if grace is obligated it is no longer grace.* The very essence of grace is that it is undeserved. God always reserves the right to have mercy upon whom he will have mercy. God may owe people justice, but never mercy.

It is important to point out once again that these problems arise for all Christians who believe in a sovereign God. These questions are not unique to a particular view of predestination.

People argue that God is loving enough to provide a way of salvation for all sinners. Since Calvinism restricts salvation only to the elect, it seems to require a less loving God. On the surface at least, it seems that a non-Calvinist view provides an opportunity for vast numbers of people to be saved who would not be saved in the Calvinist view.

Again, this question touches on matters that must be more fully developed in later chapters. For now let me say simply that, if the final decision for the salvation of fallen sinners were left in the hands of fallen sinners, we would despair of all hope that anyone would be saved.

When we consider the relationship of a sovereign God to a fallen world, we are faced with basically four options:

1. *God could decide to provide no opportunity for anyone to be saved.*
2. *God could provide an opportunity for all to be saved.*
3. *God could intervene directly and insure the salvation of all people.*
4. *God could intervene directly and insure the salvation of some people.*

All Christians immediately rule out the first option. Most Christians rule out the third. We face the problem that God saves some and not all. Calvinism answers with the fourth option. The Calvinist view of predestination teaches that God actively intervenes in the lives of the elect to make absolutely sure that they are saved. Of course the rest are invited to Christ and given an "opportunity" to be saved *if they want to*. But Calvinism assumes that without the intervention of God no one will ever want Christ. Left to themselves, no one will ever choose Christ.

This is precisely the point of dispute. Non-Reformed views of predestination assume that every fallen person is left with the capacity to choose Christ. Man is not viewed as being so fallen that it requires the direct intervention of God to the degree that Calvinism asserts. The non-Reformed views all leave it in man's power to cast the deciding ballot for man's ultimate destiny. In these views the best option is the second. God provides opportunities for all to be saved. But certainly the opportunities are not equal, since vast multitudes of people die without ever hearing the gospel.

The non-Reformed person objects to the fourth option because it limits salvation to a select group that God chooses. The Reformed person objects to the second option because he sees the universal opportunity for salvation *as not providing enough to save anybody*. The Calvinist sees God doing far more for the fallen human race through option four than through option two. The non-Calvinist sees just the reverse. He thinks that giving a universal opportunity, though it falls short of insuring the salvation of anyone, is more benevolent than insuring the salvation of some and not others.

The nasty problem for the Calvinist is seen in the relationship of options three and four. If God can and does choose to insure the salvation of some, why then does he not insure the salvation of all?

Before I try to answer that question, let me first point out that this is not just a Calvinist problem. Every Christian must feel the weight of this problem. We first face the question, "Does God have the power to insure the salvation of everyone?" Certainly it is within God's power to change the heart of every impenitent sinner and bring that sinner to himself. If he lacks such power, then he is not sovereign. If he has that power, why doesn't he use it for everyone?

The non-Reformed thinker usually responds by saying that for God to impose his power on unwilling people is to violate man's freedom. To violate man's freedom is sin. Since God cannot sin, he cannot unilaterally impose his saving grace on unwilling sinners. To force the sinner to be willing when the sinner is not willing is to violate the sinner. The idea is that by offering the grace of the gospel God does everything he can to help the sinner get saved. He has the raw power to coerce men, but the use of such power would be foreign to God's righteousness.

That does not bring much comfort to the sinner in hell. The sinner in hell must be asking, "God, if you really loved me, why didn't you coerce me to believe? I would rather have had my free will violated than to be here in this eternal place of torment." Still, the pleas of the damned would not determine God's righteousness if in fact it would be wrong of God to impose himself on the will of men. The question the Calvinist asks is, "What is wrong with God creating faith in the heart of the sinner?"

God is not required to seek the sinner's permission for doing with the sinner what he pleases. The sinner didn't ask to be born in the country of his birth, to his parents, or even to be born at all. Nor did the sinner ask to be born with a fallen nature. All these things were determined by God's sovereign decision. If God does all this that affects the sinner's eternal destiny, what could possibly be wrong for him to go one more step to insure his salvation? What did Jeremiah mean when he cried, "O Lord, You have overwhelmed me and I am overwhelmed" (see Jeremiah 20:7)? Jeremiah certainly did not invite God to overwhelm him.

The question remains. Why does God only save some? If we grant that God can save men by violating their wills, why then does he not violate everybody's will and bring them all to salvation? (I am using the word *violate* here not because I really think there is any wrongful violation but because the non-Calvinist insists on the term.)

The only answer I can give to this question is that I don't know. I have no idea why God saves some but not all. I don't doubt for a moment that God has the power to save all, but I know that he does not choose to save all. I don't know why.

One thing I do know. If it pleases God to save some and not all, there is nothing wrong with that. God is not under obligation to save anybody. If he chooses to save some, that in no way obligates him to save the rest. Again the Bible insists that it is God's divine prerogative to have mercy upon whom he will have mercy.

The hue and cry the Calvinist usually hears at this point is "That's not fair!" But what is meant by fairness here? If by fair we mean equal, then of course the protest is accurate. God does not treat all men equally. Nothing could be clearer from the Bible than that. God appeared to Moses in a way that he did not appear to Hammurabi. God gave blessings to Israel that he did not give to Persia. Christ appeared to Paul on the road to Damascus in a way he did not manifest himself to Pilate. God simply has not treated every human being in history in exactly the same manner. That much is obvious.

Probably what is meant by "fair" in the protest is "just." It does not seem just for God to choose some to receive his mercy while others do not receive the benefit of it. To deal with this problem we must do some close but very important thinking.

Let us assume that all men are guilty of sin in the sight of God. From that mass of guilty humanity, God sovereignly decides to give mercy to some of them. What do the rest get? They get justice. The saved get mercy and the unsaved get justice. Nobody gets injustice.

Mercy is not justice. But neither is it injustice. Look at the following graphic:

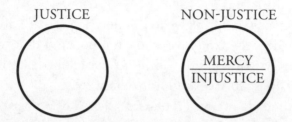

JUSTICE   NON-JUSTICE

MERCY / INJUSTICE

There is justice and there is non-justice. Non-justice includes everything outside of the category of justice. In the category of non-justice we find two sub-concepts, injustice and mercy. Mercy is a good form of non-justice while injustice is a bad form of non-justice. In the plan of salvation God does nothing bad. He never commits an injustice. Some people get justice, which is what they deserve, while other people get mercy. Again, the fact that one gets mercy does not demand that the others get it as well. God reserves the right of executive clemency.

As a human being I might *prefer* that God give his mercy to everyone equally, but I may not *demand* it. If God is not pleased to dispense his saving mercy to all men, then I must submit to his holy and righteous decision. God is never, never, never obligated to be merciful to sinners. That is the point we must stress if we are to grasp the full measure of God's grace.

The real question is why God is inclined to be merciful to anyone. His mercy is not required, yet he freely gives it to his elect.

He gave it to Jacob in a way he did not give it to Esau. He gave it to Peter in a way he did not give it to Judas. We must learn to praise God both in his mercy and in his justice. When he executes his justice he is doing nothing wrong. He is executing his justice according to his righteousness (see Romans 9:13-16).

God's Sovereignty and Human Freedom

Every Christian gladly affirms that God is sovereign. God's sovereignty is a comfort to us. It assures us that he is able to do what he promises to do. But the bare fact of God's sovereignty raises one more big question. How is God's sovereignty related to human freedom?

When we stand before the question of divine sovereignty and human freedom, the "fight or flight" dilemma may confront us. We might try to fight our way into a logical solution of it or take a turn and run as fast as we can from it.

Many of us choose to flee from it. The flight takes different routes. The most common is simply to say that divine sovereignty and human freedom are contradictions that we must have the courage to embrace. We seek analogies that soothe our troubled minds.

As a college student I heard two analogies that gave me temporary relief, like a theological package of Rolaids:

Analogy #1—"God's sovereignty and human freedom are like parallel lines that meet in eternity."

Analogy #2—"God's sovereignty and human freedom are like ropes in a well. On the surface they seem to be separate, but in the darkness of the bottom of the well they come together."

The first time I heard these analogies I was relieved. They sounded simple yet profound. The idea of two parallel lines that meet in eternity satisfied me. It gave me something clever to say in the event that a hard-boiled skeptic asked me about divine sovereignty and human freedom.

My relief was temporary. I soon required a stronger dose of Rolaids. The nagging question refused to go away. *How,* I wondered, *can parallel lines ever meet? In eternity or anywhere else?* If the lines meet, then they are not ultimately parallel. If they are ultimately parallel, then they will never meet. The more I thought about the analogy the more I realized that it did not solve the problem. To say that parallel lines meet in eternity is a nonsense statement; it is a blatant contradiction.

I don't like contradictions. I find little comfort in them. I never cease to be amazed at the ease with which Christians seem to be comfortable with them. I hear statements like, "God is bigger than logic!" or "Faith is higher than reason!" to defend the use of contradictions in theology.

I certainly agree that God is bigger than logic and that faith is higher than reason. I agree with all my heart and with all my head. What I want to avoid is a God who is smaller than logic and a faith that is lower than reason. A God who is smaller than logic would be and should be destroyed by logic. A faith that is lower than reason is irrational and absurd.

I suppose it is the tension between divine sovereignty and human freedom, more than any other issue, that has driven many Christians to claim contradictions as a legitimate element of faith. The idea is that logic cannot reconcile divine sovereignty and human freedom. The two defy logical harmony. Since the Bible teaches both poles of the contradiction we must be willing to affirm them both, in spite of the fact that they are contradictory.

God forbid! For Christians to embrace both poles of a blatant contradiction is to commit intellectual suicide and to slander the Holy Spirit. The Holy Spirit is not the author of confusion (see 1 Corinthians 14:33). God does not speak with a forked tongue.

If human freedom and divine sovereignty are real contradictions, then one of them, at least, has to go. If sovereignty excludes freedom and freedom excludes sovereignty, then either God is not sovereign or man is not free.

Happily, there is an alternative. We can keep both sovereignty and freedom if we can show that they are not contradictory.

At a human level we readily see that people can enjoy a real measure of freedom in a land ruled by a sovereign monarch. It is not freedom that is canceled out by sovereignty; it is *autonomy* that cannot coexist with sovereignty (see James 4:12).

What is autonomy? The word comes from the prefix *auto* and the root *nomos*. *Auto* means "self." An automobile is something that moves itself. "Automatic" describes something that is self-acting.

The root *nomos* is the Greek word for "law." The word *autonomy* means, then, "self-law." To be autonomous means to be a law unto oneself. An autonomous creature would be answerable to no one. He would have no governor, least of all a sovereign governor. It is logically impossible to have a sovereign God existing at the same time as an autonomous creature. The two concepts are utterly incompatible. To think of their coexistence would be like imagining the meeting of an immovable object and an irresistible force. What would happen? If the object moved, then it could no longer be considered immoveable. If it failed to move, then the irresistible force would no longer be irresistible.

So it is with sovereignty and autonomy. If God is sovereign, man cannot possibly be autonomous. If man is autonomous, God cannot possibly be sovereign. These would be contradictions.

One does not have to be autonomous to be free. Autonomy implies *absolute* freedom. We are free, but there are limits to our freedom. The ultimate limit is the sovereignty of God.

I once read a statement by a Christian who said, "God's sovereignty can never restrict human freedom." Imagine a Christian thinker making such a statement. This is sheer humanism. Does the law of God place restrictions on human freedom? Is God not permitted to impose limits on what I may choose? Not only may God impose moral limits upon my freedom, but he has every right at any moment to strike me dead if it is necessary to restrain me from exercising my evil choices. If God has no right of coercion, then he has no right of governing his creation.

It is better that we reverse the statement: "Human freedom can never restrict the sovereignty of God." That is what sovereignty is all about. If God's sovereignty is restricted by man's freedom, then God is not sovereign; man is sovereign.

God is free. I am free. God is more free than I am. If my freedom runs up against God's freedom, I lose. His freedom restricts mine; my freedom does not restrict his. There is an analogy in the human family. I have free will. My children have free wills. When our wills clash I have the authority to overrule their wills. Their wills are to be subordinate to my will; my will is not subordinate to theirs. Of course at the human level of the analogy we are not speaking in absolute terms.

Divine sovereignty and human freedom are often thought to be contradictions because on the surface they sound contradictory. There are some important distinctions that must be made and consistently applied to this question if we are to avoid hopeless confusion.

Let us consider three words in our vocabulary that are so closely related that they are often confused.

1. *contradiction*
2. *paradox*
3. *mystery*

1. Contradiction. The logical law of contradiction says that a thing cannot be what it is and not be what it is at the same time and in the same relationship. A man can be a father and a son at the same time, but he cannot be a man and not be a man at the same time. A man can be both a father and a son at the same time but not in the same relationship. No man can be his own father. Even when we speak of Jesus as the God-man we are careful to say that, though he is God and man at the same time, he is not God and man in the same relationship. He has a divine nature and a human nature. They are not to be confused. Contradictions can never coexist, not even in the mind of God. If both poles of a genuine contradiction could be true in the mind of God, then nothing God ever revealed to us could possibly have any meaning. If good and evil, justice and injustice, righteousness and unrighteousness, Christ and antichrist could all mean the same thing to God's mind, then truth of any kind would be utterly impossible.

2. Paradox. A paradox is an apparent contradiction that upon closer scrutiny can be resolved. I have heard teachers declare that the Christian notion of the Trinity is a contradiction. It simply is not. It violates no law of logic. It passes the objective test of the law of contradiction. God is one in *essence* and three in *person*. There is nothing contradictory about that. If we said that God was one in essence and three in essence then we would have a bona fide contradiction that no one could resolve. Then Christianity would be hopelessly irrational and absurd. The Trinity is a paradox, but not a contradiction.

Fogging things up even further is another term, *antinomy*. Its primary meaning is a synonym for contradiction, but its secondary meaning is a synonym for paradox. Upon examination, we see that it has the same root as *autonomy*, *nomos*, which means "law." Here the prefix is *anti*, which means "against" or "instead of." Thus the literal meaning of the term *antinomy* is "against law." What law do you suppose is in view here? The law of contradiction. The original meaning of the term was "that which violates the law of contradiction." Hence, originally and in normal philosophical discussion, the word *antinomy* is an exact equivalent of the word *contradiction*.

Confusion creeps in when people use the term *antinomy* not to refer to a genuine contradiction but to a paradox or apparent contradiction. We remember that a paradox is a statement that seems like a contradiction but actually isn't. In Great Britain, especially, the word *antinomy* is often used as a synonym for paradox.

I labor these fine distinctions for two reasons. The first is that if we are to avoid confusion we must have a clear idea in our minds of the crucial difference between a real contradiction and a seeming contradiction. It is the difference between rationality and irrationality, between truth and absurdity.

The second reason that it is necessary to state these definitions clearly is that one of the greatest defenders of the doctrine of predestination in our world today has used the term *antinomy*. I am thinking of the outstanding theologian Dr. J. I. Packer. Packer has helped countless thousands of people come to a deeper understanding of the character of God, especially with regard to God's sovereignty.

I have never discussed this matter of Dr. Packer's use of the term *antinomy* with him. I assume he is using it in the British sense of *paradox*. I cannot imagine that he means to speak of actual contradictions in the Word of God. In fact, in his book *Evangelism and the Sovereignty of God*, he labors the point that there are no ultimate contradictions in the truth of God. Dr. Packer has not only been tireless in his defense of Christian theology but has been equally tireless in his brilliant defense of the inerrancy of the Bible. If the Bible contained antinomies in the sense of real contradictions, that would be the end of inerrancy.

Some people actually do hold that there are real contradictions in divine truth. They think inerrancy is compatible with them. Inerrancy would then mean that the Bible inerrantly reveals the contradictions in God's truth without error. Of course a moment's thought would make clear that if God's truth is contradictory truth it is no truth at all. Indeed the very word *truth* would be emptied of meaning. If contradictions can be true, we would have no possible way of discerning the difference between truth and a lie. This is why I am convinced that Dr. Packer uses *antinomy* to mean paradox and not contradiction.

3. Mystery. The term *mystery* refers to that which is true but which we do not understand. The Trinity, for example, is a mystery. I cannot penetrate the mystery of the Trinity or of the incarnation of Christ with my feeble mind. Such truths are too high for me. I know that Jesus was one person with two natures, but I don't understand how that can be. The same kind of thing is found in the natural realm. Who understands the nature of gravity, or even of motion? Who has penetrated the ultimate mystery of life? What philosopher has plumbed the depths of the meaning of the human self? These are mysteries. They are not contradictions.

It is easy to confuse mystery and contradiction. We do not understand either of them. No one understands a contradiction because contradictions are intrinsically unintelligible. Not even

God can understand a contradiction. Contradictions are non-sense. No one can make sense out of them.

Mysteries are capable of being understood. The New Testament reveals to us things that were concealed and not understood in Old Testament times. There are things that once were mysterious to us that are now understood. This does not mean that everything that is presently a mystery to us will one day be made clear, but that many current mysteries will be unraveled for us. Some will be penetrated in this world. We have not yet reached the limits of human discovery. We know also that in heaven things will be revealed to us that are still hidden. But even in heaven we will not grasp fully the meaning of infinity. To understand that fully, one must himself be infinite. God can understand infinity, not because he operates on the basis of some kind of heavenly logic system, but because he himself is infinite. He has an infinite perspective.

Let me state it another way: All contradictions are mysterious. Not all mysteries are contradictions. Christianity has plenty of room for mysteries (see Deuteronomy 29:29). It has no room for contradictions. Mysteries may be true. Contradictions can never be true, neither here in our minds, nor there in God's mind.

The big issue remains. The grand debate that stirs the cauldron of controversy centers on the question, "What does predestination do to our free will?"

We will examine that issue in the next chapter.

SUMMARY OF CHAPTER 2

1. Definition of predestination.
   "Predestination means that our final destination, heaven or hell, is decided by God before we are even born."
2. God's sovereignty.
   God is supreme authority of heaven and earth.

3. God is supreme power.
   All other authority and power are under God.
4. If God is not sovereign, he is not God.
5. God exercises his sovereignty in such a way that he does no evil and violates no human freedom.
6. Man's first act of sin is a mystery. That God allowed men to sin does not reflect badly upon God.
7. All Christians face the difficult question of why God, who theoretically could save everybody, chooses to save some, but not all.
8. God does not owe salvation to anyone.
9. God's mercy is voluntary. He is not obligated to be merciful. He reserves the right to have mercy upon whom he will have mercy.

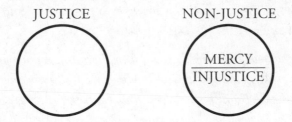

10. God's sovereignty and man's freedom are not contradictory.

For Further Study

But as for you, you meant evil against me; but God meant it for good, in order to bring it about as it is this day, to save many people alive. (GENESIS 50:20)

Since his days are determined, the number of his months is with You; you have appointed his limits, so that he cannot pass. (JOB 14:5)

Your eyes saw my substance, being yet unformed. And in Your book they all were written, the days fashioned for me, when as yet there were none of them. (PSALM 139:16)

A man's heart plans his way, but the LORD directs his steps.
   (PROVERBS 16:9)

*The lot is cast into the lap, but its every decision is from the
   LORD.* (PROVERBS 16:33)

*Remember the former things of old, for I am God, and there is
   no other; I am God, and there is none like Me, declaring the
   end from the beginning, and from ancient times things that
   are not yet done, saying, "My counsel shall stand, And I will
   do all My pleasure," Calling a bird of prey from the east, the
   man who executes My counsel, from a far country. Indeed I
   have spoken it; I will also bring it to pass. I have purposed it;
   I will also do it.* (ISAIAH 46:9-11)

*What shall we say then? Is there unrighteousness with God?
   Certainly not! For He says to Moses, "I will have mercy on
   whomever I will have mercy, and I will have compassion
   on whomever I will have compassion." So then it is not of
   him who wills, nor of him who runs, but of God who shows
   mercy.* (ROMANS 9:14-16)

CHAPTER THREE

PREDESTINATION AND FREE WILL

Predestination seems to cast a shadow on the very heart of human freedom. If God has decided our destinies from all eternity, it strongly suggests that our free choices are but charades, empty exercises in predetermined playacting. It is as though God wrote the script for us in concrete and we are merely carrying out his scenario.

To get a handle on the puzzling relationship between predestination and free will, we must first define free will. That definition itself is a matter of great debate. Probably the most common definition says *free will is the ability to make choices without any prior prejudice, inclination, or disposition.* For the will to be free it must act from a posture of neutrality, with absolutely no bias.

On the surface this is very appealing. There are no elements of coercion, either internal or external, to be found in it. Below the surface, however, lurk two serious problems. On the one hand, if we make our choices strictly from a neutral posture, with no prior inclination, then we make choices for no *reason*. If we have no reason for our choices, if our choices are utterly spontaneous, then our choices have no moral significance. If a choice just happens—it just pops out, with no rhyme or reason for it—then it cannot be judged good or bad. When God evaluates our choices, he is concerned about our motives.

Consider the case of Joseph and his brothers. When Joseph was sold into slavery by his brothers, God's providence was at work. Years later, when Joseph was reunited with his brothers in Egypt, he declared to them, "You meant evil against me; but God meant it for good" (Genesis 50:20). Here the motive was the decisive factor determining whether the act was good or evil. God's involvement in Joseph's dilemma was good; the brothers' involvement was evil. There was a reason why Joseph's brothers sold him into slavery. They had an evil motivation. Their decision was neither spontaneous nor neutral. They were jealous of their brother. Their choice to sell him was prompted by their evil desires.

The second problem this popular view faces is not so much moral as it is rational. If there is no prior inclination, desire, or bent, no prior reason for a choice, how can a choice even be made? If the will is totally neutral, why would it choose the right or the left? It is something like the problem encountered by Alice in Wonderland when she came to a fork in the road. She did not know which way to turn. She saw the grinning Cheshire Cat in the tree and asked, "Would you tell me, please, which way I ought to go from here?" To which the Cat responded, "That depends a good deal on where you want to get to." But Alice began, "I don't much care where—" "Then," said the Cat, "it doesn't matter which way you go."

Consider Alice's dilemma. Actually, she had four options from which to choose. She could have taken the left fork or the right fork. She also could have chosen to return the way she had come. Or she could have stood fixed at the spot of indecision until she died there. For her to take a step in any direction, she would need some reason or inclination to do so (which, in this case, was whatever direction led her to "somewhere"). Without any reason, any prior inclination, her only real option would be to stand there and perish.

Another famous illustration of the same problem is found in the story of the neutral-willed mule. The mule had no prior desires, or equal desires in two directions. His owner put a basket of oats to his left and a basket of wheat on his right. If the mule had no desire whatsoever for either oats or wheat he would choose neither and starve. If he had an exactly equal disposition toward oats as he had toward wheat he would still starve. His equal disposition would leave him paralyzed. There would be no motive. Without motive there would be no choice. Without choice there would be no food. Without food soon there would be no mule.

We must reject the neutral-will theory not only because it is irrational but because, as we shall see, it is radically unbiblical.

Christian thinkers have given us two very important definitions of free will. We will consider first the definition offered by Jonathan Edwards in his classic work, *On the Freedom of the Will.*

Edwards defined the will as "the mind choosing." Before we ever can make moral choices we must first have some idea of what it is we are choosing. Our selection is then based upon what the mind approves or rejects. Our understanding of values has a crucial role to play in our decision-making. My inclinations and motives as well as my actual choices are shaped by my mind. Again, if the mind is not involved, then the choice is made for no reason and with no reason. It is then an arbitrary and morally meaningless act. Instinct and choice are two different things.

A second definition of free will is "the ability to choose what we want." This rests on the important foundation of human desire. To have free will is to be able to choose according to our desires. Here desire plays the vital role of providing a motivation or a reason for making a choice.

Now for the tricky part. According to Edwards a human being is not only free to choose what he desires but he *must* choose what he desires to be able to choose at all. What I call *Edwards's Law of Choice* is this: "The will always chooses according to its strongest inclination at the moment." This means that every choice is free *and* every choice is determined.

I said it was tricky. This sounds like a blatant contradiction to say that every choice is free and yet every choice is determined. But "determined" here does not mean that some external force coerces the will. Rather it refers to one's internal motivation or desire. In shorthand the law is this: Our choices are determined by our desires. They remain our choices because they are moti-vated by our own desires. This is what we call *self-determination*, which is the essence of freedom.

Think for a minute about your own choices. How and why are they made? At this very instant you are reading the pages of this book. Why? Did you pick up this book because you have an interest in the subject of predestination, a desire to learn more about this complex subject? Perhaps. Maybe this book has been given to you to read as an assignment. Perhaps you are thinking, "I have no desire to read this whatsoever. I have to read it, and I am grimly wading through it to fulfill somebody else's desire that I read it. All things being equal, I would never choose to read this book."

But all things are not equal, are they? If you are reading this out of some kind of duty or to fulfill a requirement, you still had to make a decision about fulfilling the requirement or not fulfilling the requirement. You obviously decided that it was better or more desirable for you to read this than to leave it unread. Of that much I am sure, or you would not be reading it right now.

Every decision you make is made for a reason. The next time you go into a public place and choose a seat (in a theater, a classroom, a church building) ask yourself why you are sitting where you are sitting. Perhaps it is the only seat available and you prefer to sit rather than to stand. Perhaps you discover that there is an almost unconscious pattern emerging in your seating decisions. Maybe you discover that whenever possible you sit toward the front of the room or toward the rear. Why? Maybe it has something to do with your eyesight. Perhaps you are shy or gregarious. You may think that you sit where you sit for no reason, but the seat that you choose will always be chosen by the strongest inclination you have at the moment of decision. That inclination may merely be that the seat closest to you is free and that you don't like to walk long distances to find a place to sit down.

Decision-making is a complex matter because the options we encounter are often varied and many. Add to that that we are creatures with many and varied desires. We have different, often even conflicting, motivations.

Consider the matter of ice cream cones. Oh, do I have trouble with ice cream cones and ice cream sundaes. I love ice cream. If it is possible to be addicted to ice cream, then I must be classified as an ice cream addict. I am at least fifteen pounds overweight, and I am sure that at least twenty of the pounds that make up my body are there because of ice cream. Ice cream proves the adage to me, "A second on the lips; a lifetime on the hips." And, "Those who indulge bulge." Because of ice cream I have to buy my shirts with a bump in them.

Now, all things being equal, I would like to have a slim, trim body. I don't like squeezing into my suits and having little old ladies pat me on the tummy. Tummy-patting seems to be an irresistible temptation for some folks. I know what I have to do to get rid of those excess pounds. I have to stop eating ice cream. So I go on a diet. I go on the diet because I want to go on the diet. I want to lose weight. I desire to look better. Everything is fine until someone invites me to Swenson's. Swenson's makes the greatest "Super Sundaes" in the world. I know I shouldn't go to Swenson's. But I like to go to Swenson's. When the moment of decision comes I am faced with conflicting desires. I have a desire to be thin and I have a desire for a Super Sundae. Whichever desire is greater at the time of decision is the desire I will choose. It's that simple.

We always choose according to our strongest inclination at the moment. Even external acts of coercion cannot totally take away our freedom. Coercion involves acting with some kind of force, imposing choices upon people that, if left to themselves, they would not choose. I certainly have no desire to pay the kind of income taxes that the government makes me pay. I can refuse to pay them, but the consequences are less desirable than paying them. By threatening me with jail the government is able to impose its will upon me to pay taxes.

Or consider the case of armed robbery. A gunman steps up to me and says, "Your money or your life." He has just restricted my options to two. All things being equal, I have no desire to donate my money to him. There are far more worthy charities than he. But suddenly my desires have changed as a result of his act of external coercion. He is using force to provoke certain desires within me. Now I must choose between my desire to live and my desire to give him my money. I might as well give him the money because if he kills me he will take my money anyway.

Some people might choose to refuse, saying, "I would rather die than choose to hand this gunman my money. He'll have to take it from my dead body."

In either case, a choice is made. And it is made according to the strongest inclination at the moment. Think, if you can, of any choice you have ever made that was not according to the strongest inclination you had at the moment of decision. What about sin? Every Christian has some desire in his heart to obey Christ. We love Christ and we want to please him. Yet every Christian sins. The hard truth is that at the moment of our sin we desire the sin more strongly than we desire to obey Christ. If we always desired to obey Christ more than we desired to sin, we would never sin.

Does not the apostle Paul teach otherwise? Does he not recount for us a situation in which he acts against his desires? He says in Romans, "The good that I would, I do not: but the evil which I would not, that I do" (Romans 7:19, KJV). Here it sounds as if, under the inspiration of God the Holy Spirit, Paul is teaching clearly that there are times in which he acts against his strongest inclination.

It is extremely unlikely that the apostle is here giving us a revelation about the technical operation of the will. Rather, he is stating plainly what every one of us has experienced. We all have a desire to flee from sin. The "all things being equal" syndrome is in view here. All things being equal, I would like to be perfect. I would like to be rid of sin, just as I would like to be rid of my excess weight. But my desires do not remain constant. They fluctuate. When my stomach is full it is easy to go on a diet. When my stomach is empty my desire level changes. Temptations arise with the changing of my desires and appetites. Then I do things that, all things being equal, I would not want to do.

Paul sets before us the very real conflict of human desires, desires that yield evil choices. The Christian lives within a battlefield of conflicting desires. Christian growth involves the strengthening of desires to please Christ accompanied by the weakening of desires to sin. Paul called it the warfare between the flesh and the Spirit (see Galatians 5:17).

To say that we always choose according to our strongest inclination at the moment is to say that we always choose what we want. At every point of choice we are free and self-determined. To be self-determined is not the same thing as determinism. Determinism means that we are forced or coerced to do things by external forces. External forces can, as we have seen, severely limit our options, but they cannot destroy choice altogether. They cannot impose delight in things we hate. When that happens, when hatred turns to delight, it is a matter of persuasion, not coercion. I cannot be forced to do what I take delight in doing already.

The neutral view of free will is impossible. It involves choice without desire. That is like having an effect without a cause. It is something from nothing, which is irrational. The Bible makes it clear that we choose out of our desires. A wicked desire produces wicked choices and wicked actions. A godly desire produces godly deeds. Jesus spoke in terms of corrupt trees producing corrupt fruit. A fig tree does not yield apples and an apple tree produces no figs. So righteous desires produce righteous choices and evil desires produce evil choices (see James 3:11-12).

Moral and Natural Ability

Jonathan Edwards made another distinction that is helpful in understanding the biblical concept of free will. He distinguished between *natural ability* and *moral ability*. Natural ability has to do with the powers we receive as natural human beings. As a human being I have the natural ability to think, to walk, to talk, to see, to hear, and above all, to make choices. There are certain natural abilities that I lack. Other creatures may possess the ability to fly unaided by machines. I do not have that natural ability. I may desire to soar through the air like Superman, but I do not have this ability. The reason I cannot fly is not due to a moral deficiency in my character, but because my Creator has not given me the natural equipment necessary to fly. I have no wings.

The will is a natural ability given to us by God. We have all the natural faculties necessary to make choices. We have a mind and we have a will. We have the natural ability to choose what we desire. What, then, is our problem? According to the Bible the location of our problem is clear. It is with the nature of our desires. This is the focal point of our fallenness. Scripture declares that the heart of fallen man continually harbors desires that are only wicked (see Genesis 6:5).

The Bible has much to say about the heart of man. In Scripture the heart refers not so much to an organ that pumps blood throughout the body as it does to the core of one's being, the deepest seat of human affections. Jesus saw a close connection between the location of man's treasures and the desires of his heart. Find a man's treasure map and you have the highway of his heart (see Matthew 12:35).

Edwards declared that man's problem with sin lies with his moral ability, or lack thereof. Before a person can make a choice that is pleasing to God, he must first have a desire to please God. Before we can find God, we must first desire to seek him. Before we can choose the good, we must first have a desire for the good. Before we can choose Christ, we must first have a desire for Christ. The sum and substance of the whole debate on predestination rests squarely at this point: Does fallen man, in and of himself, have a natural desire for Christ?

Edwards answers this question with an emphatic "No!" He insists that, in the Fall, man lost his original desire for God. When he lost that desire, something happened to his freedom. He lost the moral ability to choose Christ. In order to choose Christ, the sinner must first have a desire to choose Christ. Either he has that desire already within him or he must receive that desire from God. Edwards and all who embrace the Reformed view of predestination agree that if God does not plant that desire in the human heart, then nobody, left to themselves, will ever freely choose Christ. They will always and everywhere reject the gospel, precisely because they do not desire the gospel. They will always and everywhere reject Christ because they do not desire Christ. They will freely reject Christ in the sense that they will act according to their desires.

At this point I am not trying to prove the truth of Edwards's view. To do that requires a close look at the biblical view of man's moral ability or inability. We shall do that later. We must also answer the question, "If man lacks the moral ability to choose Christ, how can God ever hold him responsible to choose Christ? If man is born in a state of moral inability, with no desire for Christ, is it not then God's fault that men do not choose Christ?" Again I beg the reader for patience, with the promise that I will take up these very important questions soon.

Augustine's View of Liberty

Just as Edwards made a crucial distinction between natural ability and moral ability, so Augustine before him made a similar distinction. Augustine got at the problem by saying that fallen man has a *free will* but lacks *liberty*. On the surface it seems like a strange distinction. How could anyone have a free will and still not have liberty?

Augustine was getting at the same thing that Edwards was. Fallen man has not lost his ability to make choices. The sinner still is able to choose what he wants; he can still act according to his desires. Yet, because his desires are corrupt he does not have the royal liberty of those set free unto righteousness. Fallen man is in a serious state of moral bondage. That state of bondage is called *original sin.*

Original sin is a very difficult subject that virtually every Christian denomination has had to face. The fall of man is so clearly taught in Scripture that we cannot construct a view of man without taking it into consideration. There are few, if any, Christians who argue that man is not fallen. Without acknowledging that we are fallen, we cannot acknowledge that we are sinners. If we do not acknowledge that we are sinners, we can hardly flee to Christ as our Savior. Admitting our fallenness is a prerequisite for coming to Christ.

It is possible to admit that we are fallen without embracing some doctrine of original sin, but only with severe difficulties in the process. It is no accident that almost every Christian body has formulated some doctrine of original sin.

At this point multitudes of Christians disagree. We agree that we must have a doctrine of original sin, but there remains great disagreement as to the concept of original sin and its extent.

Let us begin by stating what original sin is not. Original sin is not the first sin. Original sin does not refer specifically to the sin of Adam and Eve. Original sin refers to the *result* of the sin of Adam and Eve. Original sin is the punishment God gives for the first sin. It goes something like this: Adam and Eve sinned. That is the first sin. As a result of their sin humanity was plunged into moral ruin. Human nature underwent a moral fall. Things changed for us after the first sin was committed. The human race became corrupt. This subsequent corruption is what the church calls original sin.

Original sin is not a specific act of sin. It is a *condition* of sin. Original sin refers to a sin nature out of which particular sinful acts flow. Again, we commit sins because it is our nature to sin. It was not man's original nature to sin, but after the Fall, his moral nature changed. Now, because of original sin, we have a fallen and corrupt nature.

Fallen man, as the Bible declares, is born in sin. He is "under" sin. By nature we are children of wrath. We are not born in a state of innocence (see Psalm 51:5; Ephesians 2:3).

John Gerstner was once invited to preach at a local Presbyterian church. He was greeted at the door by the elders of the church, who explained that the order of worship for the day called for the administration of the sacrament of infant baptism. Dr. Gerstner agreed to perform the service. Then one of the elders explained a special tradition of the church. He asked Dr. Gerstner to present a white rose to each infant's parents before the baptism. Dr. Gerstner inquired about the meaning of the white rose. The elder replied, "We present the white rose as a symbol of the infant's innocence before God."

"I see," replied Dr. Gerstner. "And what does the water symbolize?"

Imagine the consternation of the elder when he tried to explain the symbolic purpose of washing away the sin of innocent babies. The confusion of this congregation is not unique. When we acknowledge that infants are not guilty of committing specific acts of sin it is easy to jump to the conclusion that they are therefore innocent. This is a theological broad jump into a pile of swords. Though the infant is innocent of specific acts of sin he is still guilty of original sin.

To understand the Reformed view of predestination it is absolutely necessary to understand the Reformed view of original sin. The two matters stand or fall (no pun intended) together.

The Reformed view follows the thinking of Augustine. Augustine spells out the state of Adam before the Fall and the state of mankind after the Fall. Before the Fall Adam was endowed with two possibilities: He had the ability to sin and the ability not to sin. After the Fall Adam had the ability to sin and the inability to not sin. The idea of the "inability to not" is a bit confusing to us because in English it's a double negative. Augustine's Latin formula was *non posse non peccare*. Stated another way, it means that after the Fall man was morally incapable of living without sin. The ability to live without sin was lost in the Fall. This moral inability is the essence of what we call original sin.

When we are born again, our bondage to sin is relieved. After we are made alive in Christ, we once again have the ability to sin and the ability to not sin. In heaven we will have the inability to sin.

Let's look at this with a chart:

Pre-Fall Man	*Post-Fall Man*	*Reborn Man*	*Glorified Man*
able to sin	able to sin	able to sin	
able to not sin		able to not sin	able to not sin
	unable to not sin		
			unable to sin

The chart shows that man before the Fall, after the Fall, and after being reborn is able to sin. Before the Fall he is able to not sin. This ability, the ability to not sin, is lost in the Fall. It is restored when a person is born again and continues into eternity. In creation man did not suffer from moral inability. Moral inability is a result of the Fall. To state it another way, before the Fall man was able to refrain from sinning; after the Fall man is no longer able to refrain from sinning. That is what we call original sin. This moral inability or moral bondage is overcome by spiritual rebirth. Rebirth liberates us from original sin. Before rebirth we still have a free will but we do not have this liberation from the power of sin, what Augustine called "liberty."

The person who is reborn can still sin. The ability to sin is not removed until we are glorified in heaven. We have the ability to sin but we are no longer under the bondage of original sin. We have been set free. This of course does not mean that now we live perfect lives. We still sin. But we can never say that we sin because that is all our fallen natures have the power to do.

Jesus' View of Moral Ability

We have made a brief sketch of the views of Jonathan Edwards and Augustine on the matter of moral inability. I think they are helpful and I am also persuaded that they are correct. Yet in spite of their authority as great theologians, neither of them can command from us our absolute submission to their teaching. They are both fallible. For the Christian, the teaching of Jesus is another matter. For us, and for anybody else as well if indeed Jesus is the Son of God, the teaching of Jesus must bind our consciences. His teaching on the question of man's moral ability is definitive.

One of the most important teachings of Jesus on this matter is found in the Gospel of John. "Therefore I have said to you that no one can come to Me unless it has been granted to him by My Father" (John 6:65).

Let us look closely at this verse. The first element of this teaching is a *universal negative*. The words "No one" are all-inclusive. They allow for no exception apart from the exceptions Jesus adds. The next word is crucial. It is the word *can*. This has to do with ability, not permission.

Who has not been corrected by a schoolteacher for confusing the words *can* and *may?* I used to have a teacher who never missed an opportunity to drill this point home. If I raised my hand and said, "Can I sharpen my pencil?" the response was always the same. She would smile and say, "I am sure that you can. You also *may* sharpen your pencil." The word *can* refers to ability; the word *may* refers to permission.

In this passage Jesus is not saying, "No one is allowed to come to me. . . ." He is saying, "No one is *able* to come to me. . . ."

The next word in the passage is also vital. "Unless" refers to what we call a *necessary condition*. A *necessary condition* refers to something that must happen before something else can happen.

The meaning of Jesus' words is clear. No human being can possibly come to Christ unless something happens that makes it possible for him to come. That necessary condition Jesus declares is that "it has been granted to him by the Father." Jesus is saying here that the ability to come to him is a gift from God. Man does not have the ability in and of himself to come to Christ. God must do something first.

The passage teaches at least this much: It is not within fallen man's natural ability to come to Christ on his own, without some kind of divine assistance. To this extent at least, Edwards and Augustine are in solid agreement with the teaching of our Lord.

The question that remains is this: Does God give the ability to come to Jesus to all men? The Reformed view of predestination says no. Some other views of predestination say yes. But one thing is certain; man cannot do it on his own steam without some kind of help from God.

What kind of help is required? How far must God go to overcome our natural inability to come to Christ? A clue is found elsewhere in this same chapter. In fact, there are two other statements by Jesus that have direct bearing on this question.

Earlier in chapter 6 of John's Gospel Jesus makes a similar statement. He says, "No one can come to Me unless the Father who sent Me draws him" (John 6:44). The key word here is *draw*. What does it mean for the Father to draw people to Christ? I have often heard this text explained to mean that the Father must woo or entice men to Christ. Unless this wooing takes place, no man will come to Christ. However, man has the ability to resist this wooing and to refuse the enticement. The wooing, though it is necessary, is not compelling. In philosophical language that would mean that the drawing of God is a necessary condition but not a sufficient condition to bring men to Christ. In simpler language it means that we cannot come to Christ without the wooing, but the wooing does not guarantee that we will, in fact, come to Christ.

I am persuaded that the above explanation, which is so widespread, is incorrect. It does violence to the text of Scripture, particularly to the biblical meaning of the word *draw*. The Greek word used here is *elkō*. Kittel's *Theological Dictionary of the New Testament* defines it to mean to compel by irresistible superiority. Linguistically and lexicographically, the word means "to compel."

To compel is a much more forceful concept than to woo. To

see this more clearly, let us look for a moment at two other passages in the New Testament where the same Greek word is used. In James 2:6 we read: "But you have dishonored the poor man. Do not the rich oppress you and drag you into the courts?" Guess which word in this passage is the same Greek word that elsewhere is translated by the English word *draw*. It is the word *drag*. Let us now substitute the word *woo* in the text. It would then read: "Do not the rich oppress you and *woo* you into the courts?"

The same word occurs in Acts 16:19. "But when her masters saw that their hope of profit was gone, they seized Paul and Silas and *dragged* them into the marketplace to the authorities." Again, try substituting the word *woo* for the word *drag*. Paul and Silas were not seized and then wooed into the marketplace.

I once was asked to debate the doctrine of predestination in a public forum at an Arminian seminary. My opponent was the head of the New Testament department of the seminary. At a crucial point in the debate we fixed our attention on the passage about the Father's drawing people. My opponent was the one who brought up the passage as a proof text to support his claim that God never forces anyone or compels them to come to Christ. He insisted that the divine influence on fallen man was restricted to drawing, which he interpreted to mean wooing.

At that point in the debate I quickly referred him to Kittel and to the other passages in the New Testament that translate the word *drag*. I was sure I had him. I was sure that he had walked into an insoluble difficulty for his own position. But he surprised me. He caught me completely off guard. I will never forget that agonizing moment when he cited a reference from an obscure Greek poet in which the same Greek word was used to describe the action of drawing water from a well. He looked at me and said, "Well, Professor Sproul, does one drag water from a well?"

Instantly the audience burst into laughter at this startling revelation of the alternate meaning of the Greek word. I stood there looking rather silly. When the laughter died down I replied, "No sir. I have to admit that we do not drag water from a well. But, how do we get water from a well? Do we woo it? Do we stand at the top of the well and cry, 'Here, water, water, water'?" It is as necessary for God to come into our hearts to turn us to Christ as it is for us to put the bucket in the water and pull it out if we want anything to drink. The water simply will not come on its own, responding to a mere external invitation.

As crucial as these passages from John's Gospel are, they do not surpass in importance another teaching of Jesus in the same Gospel with respect to man's moral inability. I am thinking of the famous discussion that Jesus had with Nicodemus in John 3. Jesus said to Nicodemus, "Most assuredly, I say to you, unless one is born again, he cannot see the kingdom of God" (John 3:3). Two verses later Jesus repeats the teaching: "Most assuredly, I say to you, unless one is born of water and the Spirit, he cannot enter the kingdom of God."

Once again we encounter the pivotal word *unless*. Jesus is stating an emphatic necessary precondition for any human being's ability to see and to enter the kingdom of God. That emphatic precondition is spiritual rebirth. The Reformed view of predestination teaches that before a person can choose Christ his heart must be changed. He must be born again. Non-Reformed views have fallen people first choosing Christ and then being born again. Here we find unregenerate people seeing and entering the kingdom of God. The moment a person receives Christ he is in the kingdom. One does not first believe, then become reborn, and then be ushered into the kingdom. How can a man choose a kingdom he cannot see? How can a man enter the kingdom without being first reborn? Jesus was pointing out Nicodemus's need to be born of the Spirit. He was still in the flesh. The flesh yields only flesh. The flesh, Jesus said, profits nothing. As Luther argued, "That does not mean a little something." Non-Reformed views have people responding to Christ who are not reborn. They are still in the flesh. For non-Reformed views the flesh not only profits something, it profits the most important thing a person could ever gain—entrance into the kingdom by believing on Christ. If a person who is still in the flesh, who is not yet reborn by the power of the Holy Spirit, can incline or dispose himself to Christ, what good is rebirth? This is the fatal flaw of non-Reformed views. They fail to take seriously man's moral inability, the moral impotency of the flesh.

A cardinal point of Reformed theology is the maxim: "Regeneration precedes faith." Our nature is so corrupt, the power of sin is so great, that unless God does a supernatural work in our souls we will never choose Christ. We do not believe in order to be born again; we are born again in order that we may believe.

It is ironic that in the same chapter, indeed, in the same context in which our Lord teaches the utter necessity of rebirth to even see the kingdom, let alone choose it, non-Reformed views find one of their main proof texts to argue that fallen man retains a small island of ability to choose Christ. It is John 3:16: "For God so loved the world that He gave His only begotten Son, that whoever believes in Him should not perish but have everlasting life."

What does this famous verse teach about fallen man's ability to choose Christ? The answer, simply, is *nothing*. The argument used by non-Reformed people is that the text teaches that everybody in the world has it in their power to accept or reject Christ. A careful look at the text reveals, however, that it teaches nothing of the kind. What the text teaches is that everyone who believes in Christ will be saved. Whoever does A (believes) will receive B (everlasting life). The text says nothing, absolutely nothing, about who will ever believe. It says nothing about fallen man's natural moral ability. Reformed people and non-Reformed people both heartily agree that all who believe will be saved. They heartily disagree about who has the ability to believe.

Some may reply, "All right. The text does not *explicitly* teach that fallen men have the ability to choose Christ without being reborn first, but it certainly *implies* that." I am not willing to grant that the text even implies such a thing. However, even if it did it would make no difference in the debate. Why not? Our rule of interpreting Scripture is that implications drawn from the Scripture must always be subordinate to the explicit teaching of Scripture. We must never, never, never reverse this to subordinate the explicit teaching of Scripture to possible implications drawn from Scripture. This rule is shared by both Reformed and non-Reformed thinkers.

If John 3:16 implied a universal natural human ability of fallen men to choose Christ, then that implication would be wiped out by Jesus' explicit teaching to the contrary. We have already shown that Jesus explicitly and unambiguously taught that no man has the ability to come to him without God doing something to give him that ability, namely, drawing him.

Fallen man is flesh. In the flesh he can do nothing to please God. Paul declares, "The carnal mind is enmity against God; for it is not subject to the law of God, nor indeed can be. So then, those who are in the flesh cannot please God" (Romans 8:7-8).

We ask, then, "Who are those who are 'in the flesh'?" Paul goes on to declare: "But you are not in the flesh but in the Spirit, if indeed the Spirit of God dwells in you" (Romans 8:9). The crucial word here is *if*. What distinguishes those who are in the flesh from those who are not is the indwelling of the Holy Spirit. No one who is not reborn is indwelt by God the Holy Spirit. People who are in the flesh have not been reborn. Unless they are first reborn, born of the Holy Spirit, they cannot be subject to the law of God. They cannot please God.

God commands us to believe in Christ. He is pleased by those who choose Christ. If unregenerate people could choose Christ, then they could be subject to at least one of God's commands and they could at least do something that is pleasing to God. If that is so, then the apostle has erred here in insisting that those who are in the flesh can neither be subject to God nor please him.

We conclude that fallen man is still free to choose what he desires, but because his desires are only wicked he lacks the moral ability to come to Christ. As long as he remains in the flesh, unregenerate, he will never choose Christ. He cannot choose Christ precisely because he cannot act against his own will. He has no desire for Christ. He cannot choose what he does not desire. His fall is great. It is so great that only the effectual grace of God working in his heart can bring him to faith.

SUMMARY OF CHAPTER 3

1. Free will is defined as "the ability to make choices according to our desires."
2. The concept of a "neutral free will," a will without prior disposition or inclination, is a false view of free will. It is both irrational and unbiblical.
3. True free will involves a kind of self-determination, which differs from coercion from an external force.
4. We struggle with choices, in part because we live with conflicting and changing desires.
5. Fallen man has the natural ability to make choices but lacks the moral ability to make godly choices.

6. Fallen man, as Augustine said, has "free will" but lacks "liberty."
7. Original sin is not the first sin but the sinful condition that is the *result* of Adam's and Eve's sin.
8. Fallen man is "unable to not sin."
9. Jesus taught that man is powerless to come to him without divine aid.
10. Before a person will ever choose Jesus, he must first be born again.

For Further Study

Then the LORD saw that the wickedness of man was great in the earth, and that every intent of the thoughts of his heart was only evil continually. (GENESIS 6:5)

The heart is deceitful above all things, and desperately wicked; who can know it? (JEREMIAH 17:9)

Jesus therefore answered and said to them, "Do not murmur among yourselves. No one can come to Me unless the Father who sent Me draws him; and I will raise him up at the last day." (JOHN 6:43-44)

You are of your father the devil, and the desires of your father you want to do. He was a murderer from the beginning, and does not stand in the truth, because there is no truth in him. When he speaks a lie, he speaks from his own resources, for he is a liar and the father of it. But because I tell the truth, you do not believe Me. Which of you convicts Me of sin? And if I tell the truth, why do you not believe Me? He who is of God hears God's words; therefore you do not hear, because you are not of God. (JOHN 8:44-47)

And you He made alive, who were dead in trespasses and sins. (EPHESIANS 2:1)

CHAPTER FOUR

ADAM'S FALL
AND MINE

Another difficult question that shrouds the doctrine of pre-destination is the question of how our sinful nature can be inherited from Adam. If we are born with a fallen nature, if we are born in sin, if we are born in a state of moral inability, how can God hold us responsible for our sins?

We remember that original sin does not refer to the first sin but to the result of that first sin. The Scriptures speak repeatedly of sin and death entering the world through "one man's transgression." As a result of Adam's sin, all men are now sinners. The Fall was great. It had radical repercussions for the entire human race (see Romans 5:12).

There have been many attempts to explain the relationship of Adam's fall to the rest of mankind. Some of the theories presented are quite complex and imaginative. Three theories, however, have emerged from the list as the most widely accepted. The first of these I will call "the myth theory of the Fall."

The Myth Theory of the Fall

The myth theory of the Fall, as the name suggests, holds that there was no factual, historical fall. Adam and Eve are not considered historical persons. They are mythological symbols drawn to explain or represent the problem of man's corruption. The story of the Fall in the Bible is a kind of parable; it teaches a moral lesson.

According to this theory, the first few chapters of Genesis are mythological. There never was an Adam; there never was an Eve. The very structure of the story suggests parable or myth because it includes such elements as a talking serpent and such obviously symbolic objects as the tree of knowledge of good and evil.

The moral truth communicated by the myth is that people fall into sin. Sin is a universal problem. Everyone commits sin; no one is perfect. The myth points to a higher reality: Everyone is his own Adam. Every person has his own private fall. Sin is a universal human condition precisely because every person succumbs to his own private temptation.

The attractive elements of this theory are important. In the first place, this view absolves God entirely of any responsibility for holding future generations of people responsible for what one couple did. Here, no one can blame their parents or their Creator for their own sin. In this scheme, my fallenness is a direct result of my own fall, not of someone else's.

A second advantage of this view is that it escapes all need to defend the historical character of the beginning chapters of the Bible. This view suffers no anxiety from certain theories of evolution or from scientific disputes about the nature of creation. The factual truth of a myth never needs to be defended.

The disadvantages of this view, however, are more serious. Its most crucial failing is that it actually offers nothing by way of explanation for the universality of sin. If each one of us is born without a sinful nature, how do we account for the universality of sin? If four billion people were born with no inclination to sin, with no corruption to their nature, we would reasonably expect that at least some of them would refrain from falling. If our natural moral state is one of innocent neutrality, we would statistically expect that half of the human race would remain perfect. I grant that to account for one innocent person's fall presents an enormous intellectual problem. But when we compound that difficulty by the billions of people who have fallen, the problem becomes several billion times more difficult. We also grant that if one person created in the image of God could fall, then it is indeed possible that billions can likewise fall. It is the statistical probability here that is so astonishing. When we think of one person falling, that is one thing. But if everybody does it, without exception, then we begin to wonder why. We begin to wonder if man's natural state is all that neutral.

The standard reply of the advocates of the myth view is that people are not universally born in an idyllic environment like Eden. Society is corrupt. We are born into a corrupt environment. We are like Rousseau's "innocent savage" who is corrupted by the negative influences of civilization.

This explanation begs the question. How did society or civilization get corrupt in the first place? If everyone is born innocent, without a trace of personal corruption, we would expect to find societies that are no more than half corrupt. If birds of a feather flock together, we might find societies where all the corrupt people band together and other societies where no evil is present. Society cannot be a corrupting influence until it first becomes corrupt itself. To explain the fall of an entire society or civilization, one must face the difficulties we have already pointed out.

In another one of Jonathan Edwards's famous works, his treatise on original sin, he makes the important observation that because the sin of man is universal, even if the Bible said nothing about an original Fall of the human race, reason would demand such an explanation. Nothing screams more loudly about the fact that we are born in a state of corruption than the fact that we all sin (see 1 John 1:8–10).

Another thorny question that arises concerns the relationship of sin and death. The Bible makes it clear that death is not "natural" to man. That is, death is repeatedly said to have come into the world as a result of sin. If that is so, how do we account for the death of infants? If all men are born innocent, with no innate corruption, God would be unjust to allow as yet unfallen babies to die.

The mythological view of the Fall must also face the fact that it does radical violence to the teaching of Scripture. The view does more than merely interpret the opening chapters of the Bible as non-factual. In so doing the view sets itself in clear opposition to the New Testament's view of the Fall. It would take intellectual gymnastics of the most severe sort to argue that the apostle Paul did not teach a historical Fall. The parallels that he draws between the first Adam and the second Adam are too strong to allow this, unless we argue that in Paul's mind Jesus was also a mythological character.

We grant that the Genesis account of the Fall has some unusual literary elements in it. The presence of a tree that does not follow the pattern of normal trees follows certain images of poetry. It is proper to interpret poetry as poetry and not as historical narrative. On the other hand, there are strong elements of historical narrative literature in Genesis 3. The setting of Eden is located in chapter 2 in the midst of four riverheads, including Pishon, Gihon, Hiddekel (or Tigris), and Euphrates.

We know that parables can be set in real historical settings. For example, the parable of the Good Samaritan is set in the geographical context of the road to Jericho. Therefore the mere presence of real historical rivers does not absolutely demand that we identify this section of Genesis as historical narrative.

There is another element of the text, however, that is more compelling. The account of Adam and Eve contains a significant genealogy. The Romans, with their penchant for mythology, may have no difficulty tracing their lineage to Romulus and Remus, but the Jews were surely more scrupulous about such matters. The Jews had a strong commitment to real history. In light of the vast difference between the Jewish view of history and the Greek view of history, it is unthinkable that Jewish people would include mythological characters in their own genealogies. In Jewish writing, the presence of genealogy indicates historical narrative. Note that the New Testament historian, Luke, includes Adam in the genealogy of Jesus.

It is much easier to account for a real tree serving as a focal point of a moral test and thereby being called a tree of the knowledge of good and evil than it is to accommodate genealogy to a parable or a myth. This of course could be done if other factors demanded it. But no such factors exist. There is no sound reason why we should not interpret Genesis 3 as historical narrative and multiple reasons why we should not treat it as parable or myth. To treat it as history is to treat it as the Jews did, including Paul and Jesus. To treat it otherwise is usually motivated by some contemporary agenda that has nothing to do with Jewish history.

The Realist View of the Fall

Remember the famous television series from the 1950s called *You Are There?* It took viewers, through the magic of television, to famous historical scenes. But in fact no electronic device has yet been invented to transport us back in time, H. G. Wells not-withstanding. We live in the present. Our only access to the past is through books, artifacts of archaeology, and the memories of ourselves and of others.

I remember teaching a course on the Bible that involved a brief study of Roman soldiers. I mentioned the Roman standard that carried the initials SPQR. I asked if anyone knew what those let-ters stood for. A dear friend who was in his seventies piped up, "*Senatus Populus Que Romanus*, 'The senate and the people of Rome.'" I smiled at my friend and said, "You are the only person in this room old enough to remember!"

None of us is old enough to carry memory images of the fall of Adam. Or are we? The realist view of the Fall contends that we are all old enough to remember the Fall. We should be able to remember it because we were really there.

Realism is not an exercise in a Bridey Murphy kind of reincar-nation. Rather, realism is a serious attempt to answer the problem of the Fall. The key concept is this: We cannot morally be held accountable for a sin committed by someone else. To be account-able we must have been actively involved somehow in the sin itself. Somehow we must have been present at the Fall. *Really* present. Hence the name *Realism*.

The realist view of the Fall demands some kind of concept of the preexistence of the human soul. That is, before we were born, our souls must have already existed. They were present with Adam at the Fall. They fell along with Adam. Adam's sin was not merely an act for us; it was an act *with* us. We were there.

This theory seems speculative, perhaps even bizarre. Its advo-cates, however, appeal to two pivotal biblical texts as warrant for this view. The first is found in Ezekiel 18:2-4:

"What do you mean when you use this proverb concerning the land of Israel, saying:

'The fathers have eaten sour grapes, and the children's teeth are set on edge'?

"As I live," says the Lord God, "you shall no longer use this proverb in Israel.

"Behold, all souls are Mine; The soul of the father as well as the soul of the son is Mine; The soul who sins shall die."

Later in this chapter, Ezekiel writes:

Yet you say, "Why should the son not bear the guilt of the father?" Because the son has done what is lawful and right, and has kept all My statutes and done them, he shall surely live.

The soul who sins shall die. The son shall not bear the guilt of the father, nor the father bear the guilt of the son. The righteousness of the righteous shall be upon himself, and the wickedness of the wicked shall be upon himself. (18:19-20)

Here the realist finds a definitive text for his case. God clearly declares that the son is not held guilty for the sins of his father. This would seem to pose serious difficulties for the whole idea of people falling "in Adam."

The second pivotal text for realism is found in the New Testament Book of Hebrews:

Even Levi, who receives tithes, paid tithes through Abraham, so to speak, for he was still in the loins of his father when Melchizedek met him. (7:9-10)

This text is part of a lengthy treatment by the author of Hebrews concerning the role of Christ as our Great High Priest. The New Testament declares that Jesus is both our king and our priest. It labors the fact that Jesus was from the line of Judah, to whom the royal kingdom was promised. Jesus was a son of David, who also was of the line of Judah.

The priesthood of the Old Testament was not given to Judah, but to the sons of Levi. The Levites were the priestly line. We normally speak, therefore, of the Levitical priesthood or the Aaronic priesthood. Aaron was a Levite. If this is so, how could Jesus be a priest if he was not from the line of Levi?

This problem vexed some ancient Jews. The author of Hebrews argues that there was another priesthood mentioned in the Old Testament, the priesthood of the mysterious figure named Melchizedek. Jesus is said to be a priest of the order of Melchizedek.

This lengthy portion of Hebrews is not satisfied, however, merely to prove that there was another priesthood in the Old Testament besides the Levitical priesthood. The major point of the argument here is that the priesthood of Melchizedek was *superior* to the priesthood of Levi.

The author of Hebrews rehearses a bit of Old Testament history to prove his point. He calls attention to the fact that Abraham paid tithes to Melchizedek, not Melchizedek to Abraham. Melchizedek also blessed Abraham; Abraham did not bless Melchizedek. The point is this: In the relationship between Abraham and Melchizedek it was Melchizedek who served as the priest, not Abraham.

The key thought to the Jew is cited in verse 7: "Now beyond all contradiction the lesser is blessed by the better."

The author of Hebrews continues to weave the thread of his

argument. He argues that, in effect, the father is superior to the son. That means that Abraham is ahead of Isaac in the patriarchal pecking order. In turn, Isaac is ahead of Jacob, and Jacob ahead of his sons, including his son Levi. If we carry this out, it means that Abraham is greater than his great-grandson Levi.

Now if Abraham is greater than Levi and Abraham subordinated himself to Melchizedek, then it means that the priest Melchizedek is greater than Levi and the entire line of Levi. The conclusion is clear. The priesthood of Melchizedek is a higher order of priesthood than the Levitical priesthood. This gives supreme dignity to the high priestly office of Christ.

It was not the chief concern of the author of Hebrews to explain the mystery of the fall of Adam with all this. Yet he says something along the way that the realists jump on to prove their theory. He writes that "Levi paid tithes through Abraham." Levi did this while he was "still in the loins of his father."

The realists see this reference to Levi doing something before he was even born as biblical proof for the concept of the preexistence of the human soul. If Levi could pay tithes while he was still in the loins of his father, that must mean that Levi in some sense already existed.

This treatment of this passage of Hebrews begs the question. The text does not explicitly teach that Levi really existed or preexisted in the loins of his father. The text itself calls it a "manner of speaking." The text does not demand that we leap to the conclusion that Levi "really" preexisted. The realists come to this text armed with a theory they did not find from the text and then read the theory into the text.

The argument from the text of Ezekiel also misses the point. Ezekiel was not giving a discourse on the fall of Adam. The Fall is not in view here. Rather, Ezekiel is addressing the commonplace excuse that men use for their sins. They try to blame someone else for their own misdeeds. That human activity has gone on since the Fall, but that is about all this passage has to do with the Fall. In the Fall Eve blamed the serpent, and Adam blamed both God and Eve for his own sin. He said, "The woman whom *You* gave to be with me, she gave me of the tree, and I ate" (Genesis 3:12, emphasis added).

Ever since, men have tried to pass the buck of their own guilt. Still, the realists argue, a principle is set forth in Ezekiel 18 that has bearing on the matter. The principle is that men are not held accountable for other people's sins.

To be sure, that general principle is set forth in Ezekiel. It is a grand principle of God's justice. Yet we dare not make it an absolute principle. If we do, then the text of Ezekiel would prove too much. It would prove away the atonement of Christ. If it is never possible for one person to be punished for the sins of another, then we have no Savior. Jesus was punished for our sins. That is the very essence of the gospel. Not only was Jesus punished for our sins, but his righteousness is the meritorious basis for our justification. We are justified by an alien righteousness, a righteousness that is not our own. If we press Ezekiel's statement to the absolute limit when we read, "The righteousness of the righteous shall be upon himself, and the wickedness of the wicked shall be upon himself," then we are left as sinners who must justify themselves. That puts us all in deep weeds.

To be sure, the Bible speaks of God's "visiting" the iniquities of persons on the third and fourth generations. This refers to the "fallout" or consequences of sin. A child may suffer from the consequences of his father's sin, but God does not hold him *responsible* for his father's sin.

The principle of Ezekiel allows for two exceptions: the Cross and the Fall. Somehow we don't mind the exception of the Cross. It is the Fall that rankles us. We don't mind having our guilt transferred to Jesus or having his righteousness transferred to us; it is having the guilt of Adam transferred to us that makes us howl. We argue that if the guilt of Adam had never been transmitted to us, then the work of Jesus would never have been necessary.

The Federal or Representative View of the Fall

For the most part, the federal view of the Fall has been the most popular among advocates of the Reformed view of predestination. This view teaches that Adam acted as a representative of the entire human race. With the test that God set before Adam and Eve, he was testing the whole of mankind. Adam's name means "man" or "mankind." Adam was the first human being created. He stands at the head of the human race. He was placed in the garden to act not only for himself but for all of his future descendants. Just as a federal government has a chief spokesman who is the head of the nation, so Adam was the federal head of mankind.

The chief idea of federalism is that, when Adam sinned, he sinned for all of us. His fall was our fall. When God punished Adam by taking away his original righteousness, we were all likewise punished. The curse of the Fall affects us all. Not only was Adam destined to make his living by the sweat of his brow, but that is true for us as well. Not only was Eve consigned to have pain in childbirth, but that has been true for women of all human generations. The offending serpent in the garden was not the only member of his species who was cursed to crawl on his belly.

When they were created, Adam and Eve were given dominion over the entire creation. As a result of their sin the whole world suffered. Paul tells us:

> For the creation was subjected to futility, not willingly,
> but because of Him who subjected it in hope; because the
> creation itself also will be delivered from the bondage of
> corruption into the glorious liberty of the children of God.
> For we know that the whole creation groans and labors
> with birth pangs together until now. (Romans 8:20-22)

The whole creation groans as it awaits the full redemption of man. When man sinned, the repercussions of the sin were felt throughout the whole range of man's domain. Because of Adam's sin, not only do we suffer, but lions, elephants, butterflies, and puppy dogs also suffer. They did not ask for such suffering. They were hurt by the fall of their master.

That we suffer as a result of Adam's sin is explicitly taught in the New Testament. In Romans 5, for example, Paul makes the following observations:

"Through one man sin entered the world, and death through sin" (v. 12).

"By the one man's offense many died" (v. 15).

"Through one man's offense judgment came to all men, resulting in condemnation" (v. 18).

"By one man's disobedience many were made sinners" (v. 19).

There is no way to avoid the obvious teaching of Scripture that Adam's sin had dreadful consequences for his descendants. It is precisely because of the abundance of such biblical statements that virtually every Christian body has composed some doctrine of original sin linked to the fall of Adam.

We are still left with a big question. If God did in fact judge the entire human race in Adam, how is that fair? It seems manifestly unjust of God to allow not only all subsequent human beings but all of creation to suffer because of Adam.

It is the question of God's fairness that federalism seeks to answer. Federalism assumes that we were in fact represented by Adam and that such representation was both fair and accurate. It holds that Adam *perfectly* represented us.

Within our own legal system we have situations that, not perfectly but approximately, parallel this concept of representation. We know that if I hire a man to kill someone and that hired gunman carries out the contract, I can justly be tried for first-degree murder in spite of the fact that I did not actually pull the trigger. I am judged to be guilty for a crime someone else committed because the other person acted in my place.

The obvious protest that arises at this point is, "But we did not hire Adam to sin in our behalf." That is true. This example merely illustrates that there are *some* cases in which it is just to punish one person for the crime of another.

The federal view of the Fall still exudes a faint odor of tyranny. Our cry is, "No damnation without representation!" Just as people in a nation clamor for representatives to insure freedom from despotic tyranny, so we demand representation before God that is fair and just. The federal view states that we are judged guilty for Adam's sin because he was our fair and just representative.

Wait a minute. Adam may have represented us, but we did not choose him. What if the fathers of the American republic had demanded representation from King George and the king replied, "Of course you may have representatives. You will be represented by my brother!" Such an answer would have spilled even more tea in Boston Harbor.

We want the right to select our own representatives. We want to be able to cast our own vote, not have somebody else cast that vote for us. The word *vote* comes from the Latin *votum*, which meant "wish" or "choice." When we cast our vote, we are expressing our wishes, setting forth our wills.

Suppose we would have had the total freedom to vote for our representative in Eden. Would that have satisfied us? And why do we want the right to vote for our representative? Why do we object if the king or any other sovereign wants to appoint our representatives for us? The answer is obvious. We want to be sure that our will is being carried out. If the king appoints my representative, then I will have little confidence that my wishes will be accomplished. I would fear that the appointed representative would be more eager to carry out the wishes of the king than my wishes. I would not feel fairly represented.

But even if we have the right to choose our own representatives, we have no guarantee that our wishes will be carried out. Who among us has not been enticed by politicians who promise one thing during an election campaign and do another thing after they are elected? Again, the reason we want to select our own representative is so that we can be sure we are accurately represented.

At no time in all of human history have we been more accurately represented than in the Garden of Eden. To be sure, we did not choose our representative there. Our representative was chosen for us. The one who chose our representative, however, was not King George. It was almighty God.

When God chooses our representative, he does so perfectly. His choice is an infallible choice. When I choose my own representatives, I do so fallibly. Sometimes I select the wrong person and am then inaccurately represented. Adam represented me infallibly, not because he was infallible, but because God is infallible. Given God's infallibility, I can never argue that Adam was a poor choice to represent me.

The assumption many of us make when we struggle with the Fall is that, had we been there, we would have made a different choice. We would not have made a decision that would plunge the world into ruin. Such an assumption is just not possible given the character of God. God doesn't make mistakes. His choice of my representative is greater than my choice of my own.

Even if we grant that indeed we were perfectly represented by Adam, we still must ask if it is fair to be represented at all with such high stakes. I can only answer that it pleased the Lord to do this. We know that the world fell through Adam. We know that in some sense Adam represented us. We know that we did not choose him to be our representative. We know that God's selection of Adam was an infallible selection. But was the whole process just?

I can only answer this question ultimately by asking another question—one the apostle Paul asked. "Is there unrighteousness in God?" The apostolic answer to this rhetorical question is as plain as it is emphatic. "God forbid!" (Romans 9:14).

If we know anything at all about the character of God, then we know that he is not a tyrant and that he is never unjust. His structure of the terms of mankind's probation satisfied God's own righteousness. That should be enough to satisfy us.

Yet we still quarrel. We still contend with the Almighty. We still assume that somehow God did us wrong and that we suffer as innocent victims of God's judgment. Such sentiments only confirm the radical degree of our fallenness. When we think like this, we are thinking like Adam's children. Such blasphemous thoughts only underline in red how accurately we were represented by Adam.

I am persuaded that the federal view of the Fall is substantially correct. It alone of the three we have examined does justice to the biblical teaching of the fall of man. It satisfies me that God is not an arbitrary tyrant. I know that I am a fallen creature. That is, I know that I am a creature and I know that I am fallen. I also know that it is not God's "fault" that I am a sinner. What God has done for me is to redeem me from my sin. He has not redeemed me from his sin.

Though the federal representational view of the Fall is held by most Calvinists, we must remember that the question of our relationship to Adam's fall is not a problem unique to Calvinism. All Christians must struggle with it.

It is also vital to see predestination in light of the Fall. All Christians agree that God's decree of predestination was made before the Fall. Some argue that God first predestinated some people to salvation and others to damnation and then decreed the Fall to make sure that some folks would perish. Sometimes this dreadful view is even attributed to Calvinism. Such an idea was repugnant to Calvin and is equally repugnant to all orthodox Calvinists. The notion is sometimes called "hyper-Calvinism." But even that is an insult. This view has nothing to do with Calvinism. Rather than hyper-Calvinism, it is anti-Calvinism.

Calvinism, along with other views of predestination, teaches that God's decree was made both *before* the Fall, and *in light of* the Fall. Why is this important? Because the Calvinistic view of predestination always accents the gracious character of God's redemption. When God predestines people to salvation he is predestinating people to be saved whom he knows really *need* to be saved. They need to be saved because they are sinners in Adam, not because he forced them to be sinners. Calvinism sees Adam sinning by his own free will, not by divine coercion.

To be sure, God knew before the Fall that there would most certainly be a fall and he took action to redeem some. He ordained the Fall in the sense that he chose to allow it, but not in the sense that he chose to coerce it. His predestinating grace is gracious precisely because he chooses to save people whom he knows in advance will be spiritually dead.

One final illustration may be helpful here. We bristle at the idea that God calls us to be righteous when we are hampered by original sin. We say, "But God, we can't be righteous. We are fallen creatures. How can you hold us accountable when you know very well we were born with original sin?"

The illustration is as follows. Suppose God said to a man, "I want you to trim these bushes by three o'clock this afternoon. But be careful. There is a large open pit at the edge of the garden. If you fall into that pit, you will not be able to get yourself out. So whatever you do, stay away from that pit."

Suppose that as soon as God leaves the garden the man runs over and jumps into the pit. At three o'clock God returns and finds the bushes untrimmed. He calls for the gardener and hears a faint cry from the edge of the garden. He walks to the edge of the pit and sees the gardener helplessly flailing around on the bottom. He says to the gardener, "Why haven't you trimmed the bushes I told you to trim?" The gardener responds in anger, "How do you expect me to trim these bushes when I am trapped in this pit? If you hadn't left this empty pit here, I would not be in this predicament."

Adam jumped into the pit. In Adam we all jumped into the pit. God did not throw us into the pit. Adam was clearly warned about the pit. God told him to stay away. The consequences Adam experienced from being in the pit were a direct punishment for jumping into it.

So it is with original sin. Original sin is both the consequence of Adam's sin and the punishment for Adam's sin. We are born sinners because in Adam we all fell. Even the word *fall* is a bit of a euphemism. It is a rose-colored view of the matter. The word *fall* suggests an accident of sorts. Adam's sin was not an accident. He was not Humpty Dumpty. Adam didn't simply slip into sin; he jumped into it with both feet. We jumped headlong with him. God didn't push us. He didn't trick us. He gave us adequate and fair warning. The fault is ours and only ours.

It is not that Adam ate sour grapes and our teeth are set on edge. The biblical teaching is that in Adam we all ate the sour grapes. That is why our teeth are set on edge.

SUMMARY OF CHAPTER 4

1. The pervasive, universal presence of human sin cannot be explained adequately by a myth.
2. Man's sinfulness cannot be explained by "society."
3. Society is made up of individual persons, who each must be a sinner before the society as a whole can be corrupt.
4. Realism also fails as an explanation because it involves speculative exegesis of Scripture.
5. The federal view of the Fall takes seriously the role Adam played as our representative.
6. Adam perfectly represented us not by virtue of his perfection but by virtue of God's perfect selection.
7. All Christians must have some view of the Fall.
8. God's saving grace is directed toward those whom he knows to be fallen creatures.

For Further Study

> So when the woman saw that the tree was good for food, that it was pleasant to the eyes, and a tree desirable to make one wise, she took of its fruit and ate. She also gave to her husband with her, and he ate. Then the eyes of both of them were

*opened, and they knew that they were naked; and they sewed
fig leaves together and made themselves coverings.*
(GENESIS 3:6-7)

*Behold, I was brought forth in iniquity, and in sin my mother
conceived me.* (PSALM 51:5)

*For I desire mercy and not sacrifice, and the knowledge of God
more than burnt offerings. But like men [Adam] they trans-
gressed the covenant; there they dealt treacherously with Me.*
(HOSEA 6:6-7)

*Again, the devil took Him up on an exceedingly high mountain,
and showed Him all the kingdoms of the world and their
glory. And he said to Him, "All these things I will give You if
You will fall down and worship me." Then Jesus said to him,
"Away with you, Satan! For it is written, 'You shall worship
the LORD your God, and Him only you shall serve.'" Then
the devil left Him, and behold, angels came and ministered
to Him.* (MATTHEW 4:8-11)

*As by one man's disobedience many were made sinners, so also by
one Man's obedience many will be made righteous.*
(ROMANS 5:19)

*For since by man came death, by Man also came the resurrection
of the dead. For as in Adam all die, even so in Christ all shall
be made alive.* (1 CORINTHIANS 15:21-22)

*As was the man of dust, so also are those who are made of
dust; and as is the heavenly Man, so also are those who are
heavenly. And as we have borne the image of the man of dust,
we shall also bear the image of the heavenly Man.*
(1 CORINTHIANS 15:48-49)

CHAPTER FIVE

SPIRITUAL DEATH AND SPIRITUAL LIFE: REBIRTH AND FAITH

Reformed theology is famous for a simple acrostic that was designed to summarize the so-called "Five Points of Calvinism." It spells the word *TULIP*.

T—Total Depravity
U—Unconditional Election
L—Limited Atonement
I—Irresistible Grace
P—Perseverance of the Saints

This acrostic has helped many people remember the distinguishing characteristics of Reformed theology. Unfortunately, it has also caused great confusion and much misunderstanding. The problem with acrostics is that the best terms we have for ideas don't always start with letters that will spell neat, little words. The acrostic serves well as a memory device, but that is about it.

My first problem with the acrostic TULIP is with the first

letter. *Total depravity* is a very misleading term. The concept of total depravity is often confused with the idea of utter depravity. In Reformed theology total depravity refers to the idea that our *whole humanity* is fallen. That is, there is no part of me that has not been affected in some way by the Fall. Sin affects my will, my heart, my mind, and my body. If Adam had never sinned, I suppose he would not have had the need to wear bifocals when he reached middle age. In fact the very term *middle age* would have been meaningless to him. Had he not sinned, Adam would not have died. When one lives forever, where is middle age?

Total depravity also stresses the fact that sin reaches to the core of our being. Sin is not a peripheral thing, a slight blemish that mars an otherwise perfect specimen. Sin is *radical* in the sense that it touches the root (*radix*) of our lives.

Total depravity is not utter depravity. Utter depravity would mean that we are all as sinful as we possibly could be. We know that is not the case. No matter how much each of us has sinned, we are able to think of worse sins that we could have committed. Even Adolf Hitler refrained from murdering his mother.

Since total depravity is often confused with utter depravity, I prefer to speak of the "radical corruption" of man. That does mess up our acrostic. What in the world is a rulip? The concept of the radical character of sin is perhaps the most important concept for us to understand if we are going to make any sense out of the biblical doctrine of predestination. As I mentioned during our discussion of man's moral inability, this is the focal point of the entire debate.

I remember teaching a college class in theology. The class was made up of an interdenominational group of about twenty-five students. I asked at the beginning of the study on predestination how many students considered themselves Calvinists on the matter. Only one student raised his hand.

We started with a study of man's sinfulness. After I lectured for several days on the subject of man's corruption I took another poll. I asked, "How many of you are persuaded that what you have just learned is in fact the Bible doctrine of human sinfulness?" Every hand went up. I said, "Are you sure?" They insisted that they were indeed sure. I gave a further warning. "Be careful now. This may come back to haunt you later in the course." No matter. They insisted that they were convinced.

At this point in the class I went to the corner of the chalkboard and wrote the date. Next to the date I wrote the figure 25. I put a circle around this and added a note to the janitor to please refrain from erasing this portion of the board.

Several weeks later we began a study of predestination. When I got to the point of man's moral inability there were howls of protest. Then I went to the chalkboard and reminded them of the earlier poll. It took another two weeks to convince them that, if they really accepted the biblical view of human corruption, the debate about predestination for all intents and purposes was already over.

I shall, in brief, attempt to do the same thing here. I proceed with the same caution.

The Biblical View of Human Corruption

Let us begin our study of the degree of man's fallenness by looking at Romans 3. Here the apostle Paul writes:

There is none righteous, no, not one;
There is none who understands;
There is none who seeks after God.

They have all gone out of the way;
They have together become unprofitable;
There is none who does good, no, not one
(ROMANS 3:10-12)

Here we find a brief summation of the universality of human corruption. Sin is so pervasive that it captures everyone in its net. Paul uses words of emphasis to show that there are no exceptions to this indictment among fallen men. There is none righteous; there is none who does good.

The statement "There is none who does good, no, not one" flies in the face of our cultural assumptions. We grow up hearing that nobody is perfect and that to err is human. We are quite willing to acknowledge that none of us is perfect. That we are sinners is easy to admit; that none of us even does good is a bit much. Not one person in a thousand will admit that sin is this serious.

No one does good? How can that be? Every day we see rank pagans doing some good. We see them performing heroic acts of sacrifice, works of industry, prudence, and honesty. We see unbelievers scrupulously obeying the speed limits while cars whiz by them bearing bumper stickers that read, "Honk if you love Jesus."

Paul must be using hyperbole here. He must be intentionally exaggerating in order to make a point. Surely there are people who do good. No! The sober judgment of God is that no one does good, no, not one.

We stumble here because we have a relative understanding of what good is. Good is, indeed, a relative term. Something can only be judged good according to some sort of standard. We use the term as a comparison among men. When we say that a man is good, we mean that he is good compared with other men. But the ultimate standard for goodness, the standard by which we shall all be judged, is the law of God. That law is not God, but it comes from God and reflects the perfect character of God himself. Judged against that standard, no one is good.

In biblical categories a good deed is measured in two parts. The first is in its outward conformity to the law of God. This means that, if God prohibits stealing, then it is good not to steal. It is good to tell the truth. It is good to pay our bills on time. It is good to assist people in need. Outwardly these virtues are performed every day. When we see them we quickly conclude that men do in fact do good things.

It is the second part of the measuring that gets us in trouble. Before God pronounces a deed "good" he considers not only the outward or external conformity to his law, but also the motivation. We look only at outward appearances; God reads the heart. For a work to be considered good it must not only conform outwardly to the law of God, but it must be motivated inwardly by a sincere love for God.

We remember the Great Commandment to love the Lord our God with all our hearts, all our strength, and all our minds . . . and love our neighbors as much as we love ourselves. Every deed that we do should proceed from a heart that loves God totally (see Matthew 22:37-39).

From this perspective it is easy to see that no one does good. Our best works are tainted by our less than pure motives. No one among us has ever loved God with all of his heart or with all of his mind. There is a pound of flesh mixed in with all of our deeds, rendering them less than perfect.

Jonathan Edwards spoke of the concept of *enlightened self-interest*. Enlightened self-interest refers to that motivation we all feel to perform external righteousness and to restrain some evil impulses within ourselves. There are certain times and places where crime does not pay. Where the risk of punishment outweighs the possible reward of our misdeed, we may be inclined to refrain from it. On the other hand, we may win the applause of men by our virtuous acts. We may gain a pat on the head from our teacher or the respect of our peers if we do certain good deeds.

The whole world applauds recording artists when they band together to produce a special album with the proceeds to be used to relieve famine in Ethiopia or devastation in Haiti. Applause rarely hurts the career of a stage performer, despite cynical statements that ethics and business do not mix. On the contrary, most of us have learned that ethics enhance our reputations in business.

I am not so cynical as to think that gestures for the Third World by singers are done purely for personal applause or as a publicity stunt. Surely there are strong motives of compassion and care for hurting people. On the other hand, I am not so naïve as to think that such motives are totally without self-interest. The compassion may far outweigh the self-interest, but no matter how minuscule, there is at least a grain of self-interest mixed in. There always is, in all of us. If we deny this I suspect that our very denials are motivated in part by self-interest.

We want to deny this allegation. We sense in our own hearts at times an overwhelming feeling of performing from duty alone. We like to think that we are truly altruistic. But no one ever flatters us more than we flatter ourselves. The weight of our motives may at times lean heavily in the direction of altruism, but it is never perfectly there.

God does not grade on a curve. He demands perfection. None of us performs to that level. We do not do what God commands.

Ever. Therefore the apostle is not indulging himself with hyperbole. His judgment is accurate. There is none who does good, no, not one. Jesus himself reinforced this view in his discussion with the rich young ruler. "No one is good but One, that is, God" (Luke 18:19).

As troublesome as this indictment is, another element in the Romans passage may bring even more consternation to us, especially to evangelical Christians who talk and think to the contrary. Paul says, "There is none who seeks after God."

How many times have you heard Christians say, or have you heard the words from your own mouth, "So and so is not a Christian, but he's searching"? It is a common statement among Christians. The idea is that there are people all over the place who are searching for God. Their problem is that they just haven't been able to find him. He is playing hide and seek. He is elusive.

In the Garden of Eden when sin came into the world, who hid? Jesus came into the world to *seek* and to save the lost. Jesus wasn't the one who was hiding. God is not a fugitive. We are the ones on the run. Scripture declares that the wicked flee when no man pursues (see Proverbs 28:1). As God through Moses said, "The sound of a shaken leaf shall cause them to flee" (Leviticus 26:36). The uniform teaching of Scripture is that fallen men are fleeing from God. There is none who seeks after God.

Why is it, then, despite such clear biblical teaching to the contrary, that Christians persist in claiming that they know people who are searching for God but have not yet found him? Thomas Aquinas shed some light on this. Aquinas said that we confuse two similar yet different human actions. We see people searching desperately for peace of mind, relief from guilt, meaning and purpose to their lives, and loving acceptance. We know that ultimately these things can only be found in God. Therefore we conclude that since people are seeking these things they must be seeking after God.

People do not seek God. They seek after the *benefits that only God can give them*. The sin of fallen man is this: Man seeks the benefits of God while at the same time fleeing from God himself. We are, by nature, fugitives.

The Bible tells us repeatedly to seek after God. The Old Testament cries, "Seek the Lord while He may be found" (Isaiah 55:6). Jesus said, "Seek, and you will find; knock, and it will be opened to you" (Matthew 7:7). The conclusion we draw from these texts is that since we are called to seek after God it must mean that we, even in our fallen state, have the moral capacity to do that seeking. But who is being addressed in these texts? In the case of the Old Testament it is the people of Israel who are called to seek the Lord. In the New Testament it is believers who are called to seek the kingdom.

We have all heard evangelists quote from Revelation: "I stand at the door and knock. If anyone hears My voice and opens the door, I will come in to him and dine with him, and he with Me" (Revelation 3:20). Usually the evangelist applies this text as an appeal to the unconverted, saying, "Jesus is knocking at the door of your heart. If you open the door he will come in." In the original saying, however, Jesus directed his remarks to the church. It was not an evangelistic appeal.

So what? The point is that seeking is something that unbelievers do not do on their own steam. *The unbeliever will not seek. The unbeliever will not knock.* Seeking is the business of believers. Edwards said, "The seeking of the kingdom of God is the chief business of the Christian life." Seeking is the result of faith, not the cause of it.

When we are converted to Christ, we use language of discovery to express our conversion. We speak of finding Christ. We may have a bumper sticker that reads I FOUND IT. These statements are indeed true. The irony is this: Once we have found Christ it is not the end of our seeking, but the beginning. Usually, when we find what we are looking for, it signals the end of our searching. But when we "find" Christ, it is the beginning of our search. The Christian life begins at conversion; it does not end where it begins. It grows; it moves from faith to faith, from grace to grace, from life to life. This movement of growth is prodded by a continual seeking after God.

There is one more insight in Romans 3 that we need to look at briefly. Not only does the apostle declare that no one seeks after God, but he adds the thought, "They have together become unprofitable." We must remember that here Paul is speaking of fallen men, natural men, unconverted men. This is a description of people who are still in the flesh.

What does Paul mean by unprofitable? Jesus earlier spoke of unprofitable servants. Profit has to do with positive values. The unconverted person, working in the flesh, achieves nothing of permanent value. In the flesh he may gain the whole world but he loses the thing of most value to himself, his own soul. The most valuable possession a person can ever have is Christ. He is the pearl of great price. To have him is to have the greatest possible profit.

The person who is spiritually dead cannot, in his own flesh, gain the profit of Christ. He is described as one who has no fear of God before his eyes (see Romans 3:18). Those who are not righteous, who do no good, who never seek after God, who are altogether unprofitable, and who have no fear of God before their eyes, never incline their own hearts to Christ.

Quickening from Spiritual Death

The cure for spiritual death is the creation of spiritual life in our souls by God the Holy Spirit. A summary of this work is given to us in Ephesians:

> And you He made alive, who were dead in trespasses and sins, in which you once walked according to the course of this world, according to the prince of the power of the air, the spirit who now works in the sons of disobedience, among whom also we all once conducted ourselves in the lusts of our flesh, fulfilling the desires of the flesh and of the mind, and were by nature children of wrath, just as the others.
>
> But God, who is rich in mercy, because of His great love with which He loved us, even when we were dead in trespasses, made us alive together with Christ (by grace you have been saved), and raised us up together, and made us sit together in the heavenly places in Christ Jesus, that in the ages to come He might show the exceeding riches of His grace in His kindness toward us in Christ Jesus.
>
> For by grace you have been saved through faith, and that not of yourselves; it is the gift of God, not of works, lest any man should boast. For we are His workmanship, created in Christ Jesus for good works, which God prepared beforehand that we should walk in them. (Ephesians 2:1-10)

Here we find a predestinarian passage par excellence. Notice that throughout this passage Paul places a heavy accent on the riches of God's grace. We must never shortchange this grace. The passage celebrates the newness of life that the Holy Spirit has created in us.

This work of the Spirit is sometimes called quickening. Rarely heard in ordinary speech, the term is almost exclusively used to describe an event that happens during a pregnancy. "Quickening" refers to the woman's first feeling of the life of the baby she is carrying in her womb.

What is here called quickening or being made alive is what is elsewhere called rebirth or regeneration. The term *regeneration*, as the word suggests, indicates a "generating again." To generate means to cause to happen or to begin. We think of the first book of the Bible, the book of beginnings, which is called Genesis. The prefix *re-* means simply "again." Therefore the word *regeneration* means to begin something again. It is the new beginning of life that we are concerned with here, the beginning of spiritual life.

We note that this image of life is contrasted with an image of death. Fallen man is here described as being "dead in sin." In order for one who is dead to the things of God to come alive to God, something must be done *to* him and *for* him. Dead men cannot make themselves come alive. Dead men cannot create spiritual life within themselves. Paul makes it crystal clear here that it is God who makes alive; it is God who quickens us from spiritual death.

Fallen man is dead in sin. He is described here as being "by nature, a child of wrath." His fallen pattern is to "walk according to the course of this world." His allegiance is not to God but to the prince of the power of the air. Paul states that this is not merely the state of all the worst sinners but the former state of himself and of his brothers and sisters in Christ. ("Among whom also we all once conducted ourselves in the lusts of our flesh, fulfilling the desires of the flesh. . . .")

Most non-Reformed views of predestination fail to take seriously the fact that fallen man is spiritually dead. Other evangelical positions acknowledge that man is fallen and that his fallenness is a serious matter. They even grant that sin is a radical problem. They are quick to grant that man is not merely ill, but mortally ill, sick unto death. But he has not quite died yet. He still has one tiny breath of spiritual life left in his body. He still has a tiny island of righteousness left in his heart, a tiny and feeble moral ability that abides in his fallenness.

I have heard two illustrations from evangelists who plead for the repentance and conversion of their hearers. The first is an analogy of a person suffering from a terminal illness. The sinner is said to be gravely ill, on the very brink of death. He does not have it within his own power to cure himself of the disease. He is lying on his deathbed almost totally paralyzed. He cannot recover unless God provides the healing medicine. The man is so bad off that he cannot even stretch forth his arm to receive the medicine. He is almost comatose. God must not only offer the medicine but God must put it on a spoon and place it by the dying man's lips. Unless God does all that, the man will surely perish. But though God does 99 percent of what is necessary, the man is still left with one percent. He must open his mouth to receive the medicine. This is the necessary exercise of free will that makes the difference between heaven and hell. The man who opens his mouth to receive the gracious gift of the medicine will be saved. The man who keeps his lips tightly clenched will perish.

This analogy *almost* does justice to the Bible and to Paul's teaching of the grace of regeneration. But not quite. The Bible does not speak of mortally ill sinners. According to Paul they are *dead*. There is not an ounce of spiritual life left in them. If they are to be made alive, God must do more than offer them medicine. Dead men will not open their mouths to receive anything. Their jaws are locked in death. Rigor mortis has set in. They must be raised from the dead. They must be new creations, crafted by Christ and reborn by his Spirit.

A second illustration is equally popular with those committed to evangelism. In this view fallen man is seen as a drowning man who is unable to swim. He has gone under twice and bobbed to the surface for the last time. If he goes under again he will die. His only hope is for God to throw him a life preserver. God throws the lifeline and tosses it precisely to the edge of the man's outstretched fingers. All the man has to do to be saved is to grab hold. If he will only grab hold of the life preserver, God will tow him in. If he refuses the life preserver, he will certainly perish.

Again, in this illustration the utter helplessness of sinful man without God's assistance is emphasized. The drowning man is in a serious condition. He cannot save himself. However, he is still alive; he can still stretch forth his fingers. His fingers are the crucial link to salvation. His eternal destiny depends upon what he does with his fingers.

Paul says the man is dead. He is not merely drowning, he has already sunk to the bottom of the sea. It is futile to throw a life preserver to a man who has already drowned. If I understand Paul, I hear him saying that God dives into the water and pulls a dead man from the bottom of the sea and then performs a divine act of mouth-to-mouth resuscitation. He breathes into the dead man new life.

It is important to remember that regeneration has to do with new life. It is called the new birth or being born again. Much confusion exists about this matter. The new birth is closely linked in the Bible to the new life that is ours in Christ. Just as in natural biology there can be no life without birth, so in supernatural terms there can be no new life without a new birth.

Birth and life are closely connected but they are not exactly the same thing. Birth is the beginning of the new life. It is a decisive moment. We understand that in normal biological terms. Every year we celebrate our birthdays. We are not like the queen in *Alice in Wonderland* who celebrated all of her "unbirthdays." Birth is a one-time experience. It may be celebrated but not repeated. It is a decisive moment of transition. A person is either born or not yet born.

So it is with spiritual rebirth. Rebirth produces new life. It is the beginning of new life but it is not the total sum of the new life. It is the crucial point of transition from spiritual death to spiritual life. A person is never partially born again. He is either regenerate or he is not regenerate.

The clear biblical teaching of regeneration is that it is the work of God and the work of God alone. We cannot cause ourselves to be reborn. The flesh cannot produce the spirit. Regeneration is an act of *creation*. God does the creating.

In theology we have a technical term that may be helpful, *monergism*. It comes from two root words. *Mono* means "one." A monopoly is a business that has the market to itself. A monoplane is a single-winged aircraft. *Erg*, you may remember from grade school, refers to a unit of work. We get the common word *energy* from it.

Putting the parts together, we get the meaning "one working." When we say that regeneration is monergistic, we mean that only one party is doing the work. That party is God the Holy Spirit. He regenerates us; we cannot do it ourselves or even help him with the task.

It may sound as if we are treating human beings like puppets. Puppets are made of wood. They can make no response. They are inert, lifeless. They are moved about by strings. But we are not talking about puppets. We are talking about humans who are spiritual corpses. These humans do not have hearts made of sawdust; they are made of stone. They are not manipulated by strings. They are biologically alive. They act. They make decisions, but never decisions for God.

When God regenerates a human soul, when he makes us spiritually alive, we make choices. We believe. We have faith. We cling to Christ. God does not believe for us. Faith is not monergistic.

Earlier we talked about the plight of fallen man and the status of his human will. We affirmed that though he is fallen he still has a free will in the sense that he can still make choices. His problem, which we defined as moral inability, is that he lacks a desire for Christ. He is indisposed and disinclined toward Christ. Unless or until man is inclined to Christ he will never choose Christ. Unless he first desires Christ, he will never receive Christ.

In regeneration, God changes our hearts. He gives us a new disposition, a new inclination. He plants a desire for Christ in our hearts. We can never trust Christ for our salvation unless we first desire him. This is why we said earlier that *regeneration precedes faith*. Without rebirth we have no desire for Christ. Without a desire for Christ we will never choose Christ. Therefore we conclude that before anyone ever will believe, before anyone *can* believe, God must first change the disposition of his heart.

When God regenerates us, it is an act of grace. Let us look again at Ephesians 2: "But God, who is rich in mercy, because of His great love with which He loved us, even when we were dead in trespasses, made us alive. . . ."

I have a sign on my desk that was embroidered for me by a woman in a church I once served. The sign reads simply, "But." When Paul rehearses fallen man's spiritual condition, it is enough to drive us to despair. Finally he gets to the magic word that makes us breathe a sigh of relief. But. Without it we are doomed to perish. The "but" captures the essence of the good news.

Paul says, "But God, who is rich in mercy. . . ." Notice that he does not say, "But man, who is rich in goodness." It is God alone who makes us alive. When does he do it? Paul does not leave us to guess. He says, ". . . when we were dead in trespasses." This is the amazing part of grace, that it is given to us when we are spiritually dead.

Paul concludes that it is a matter of grace and not a matter of works. His sterling summary is, "For by grace you have been saved through faith, and that not of yourselves, it is the gift of God." This passage should seal the matter forever. The faith by which we are saved is a gift. When the apostle says it is not of ourselves, he does not mean that it is not our faith. Again, God does not do the believing for us. It is our own faith but it does not originate with us. It is given to us. The gift is not earned or deserved. It is a gift of sheer grace.

During the Protestant Reformation there were three slogans that became famous. They are Latin phrases: *sola fide, sola grátia,* and *soli Deo gloria.* The three slogans belong together. They ought never to be divorced from one another. They mean, "by faith alone," "by grace alone," and "to God alone the glory."

Irresistible Grace?

Most Christians agree that God's work of regeneration is a work of grace. The issue that divides us is whether or not this grace is irresistible. Is it possible for a person to receive the grace of regeneration and still not come to faith?

The Calvinist answers with an emphatic "No!"—but not because he believes that God's saving grace is literally irresistible.

Again we run into a problem with the old acrostic TULIP. We have already changed the tulip to rulip and now we are going to have to change it some more. Now we will call it "rulep."

The term *irresistible grace* is misleading. Calvinists all believe that men can and do resist the grace of God. The question is, "Can the grace of regeneration fail to accomplish its purpose?" Remember that spiritually dead people are still biologically alive. They still have a will that is disinclined toward God. They will do everything in their power to resist grace. The history of Israel is the history of a hardhearted and stiff-necked people who resisted God's grace repeatedly.

God's grace is resistible in the sense that we can and do resist it. It is irresistible in the sense that it achieves its purpose. It brings about God's desired effect. Thus I prefer the term *effectual grace*.

We are speaking of the grace of regeneration. We remember that in regeneration God creates in us a desire for himself. But when we have that desire planted in us, we will continue to function as we always have functioned, making our choices according to the strongest motivation at the moment. If God gives us a desire for Christ we will act according to that desire. We will most certainly choose the object of that desire; we will choose Christ. When God makes us spiritually alive we become spiritually alive. It is not merely the possibility of becoming spiritually alive that God creates. He creates spiritual life within us. When he calls something into being, it comes into being.

We speak of the *inward call* of God. The inward call of God is as powerful and effective as his call to create the world. God did not invite the world into existence. By divine mandate he called out, "Let there be light!" And there was light. It could not have been otherwise. The light *had* to begin to shine.

Could Lazarus have stayed in the tomb when Jesus called him out? Jesus cried, "Lazarus, come forth!" (John 11:43–44). The man broke out of his grave clothes and came out of the tomb. When God creates, he exercises a power that only God has. He alone has the power to bring something out of nothing and life out of death.

Much confusion exists on this point. I remember the first lecture I ever heard from John Gerstner. It was on the subject of predestination. Shortly into his lecture Dr. Gerstner was interrupted by a student who was waving his hand in the air. Gerstner stopped and acknowledged the student. The student asked, "Dr. Gerstner, is it safe to assume that you are a Calvinist?" Gerstner answered, "Yes," and resumed his lecture. A few moments later a gleam of recognition appeared in Gerstner's eyes and he stopped speaking in mid-sentence and asked the student, "What is your definition of a Calvinist?"

The student replied, "A Calvinist is someone who believes that God forces some people to choose Christ and prevents other people from choosing Christ." Gerstner was horrified. He said, "If that is what a Calvinist is, then you can be sure that I am not a Calvinist."

The student's misconception of irresistible grace is widespread. I once heard the president of a Presbyterian seminary declare, "I am not a Calvinist because I do not believe that God brings some people, kicking and screaming against their wills, into the kingdom, while he excludes others from his kingdom who desperately want to be there."

I was astonished when I heard these words. I did not think it possible that the president of a Presbyterian seminary could have such a gross misconception of his own church's theology. He was reciting a caricature which was as far away from Calvinism as one could get.

Calvinism does not teach and never has taught that God brings people kicking and screaming into the kingdom or has ever excluded anyone who wanted to be there. Remember that the cardinal point of the Reformed doctrine of predestination rests on the biblical teaching of man's spiritual death. Natural man does not want Christ. He will only want Christ if God plants a desire for Christ in his heart. Once that desire is planted, those who come to Christ do not come kicking and screaming against their wills. They come because they want to come. They now desire Jesus. They rush to the Savior. The whole point of irresistible grace is that rebirth quickens someone to spiritual life in such a way that Jesus is now seen in his irresistible sweetness. Jesus is irresistible to those who have been made alive to the things of God. Every soul whose heart beats with the life of God within it longs for the living Christ. All whom the Father gives to Christ come to Christ (see John 6:37).

The term *effectual grace* may help to avoid some confusion. Effectual grace is grace that effects what God desires.

How does this view differ from other non-Reformed views of regeneration? The most popular alternate view rests upon the concept of prevenient grace.

Prevenient Grace

As the name suggests, prevenient grace is grace that "comes before" something. It is normally defined as a work that God does for everybody who responds to him. He gives all people enough grace to respond to Jesus. That is, it is enough grace to make it *possible* for people to choose Christ. Those who cooperate with and assent to this grace are "elect." Those who refuse to cooperate with this grace are lost.

The strength of this view is that it recognizes that fallen man's spiritual condition is severe enough that it requires God's grace to save him. The weakness of the position may be seen in two ways. If this prevenient grace is merely external to man, then it fails in the same manner that the medicine and the life preserver analogies fail. What good is prevenient grace if offered outwardly to spiritually dead creatures?

On the other hand, if prevenient grace refers to something that God does within the heart of fallen man, then we must ask why it is not always effectual. Why is it that some fallen creatures choose to cooperate with prevenient grace and others choose not to? Doesn't everyone get the same amount?

Think of it this way, in personal terms. If you are a Christian you are surely aware of other people who are not Christians. Why is it that you have chosen Christ and they have not? Why did you say yes to prevenient grace while they said no? Was it because you were more righteous than they were? If so, then indeed you have something in which to boast. Was that greater righteousness something you achieved on your own or was it the gift of God? If it was something you achieved, then at the bottom line your salvation depends on your own righteousness. If the righteousness was a gift, then why didn't God give the same gift to everybody?

Perhaps it wasn't because you were more righteous. Perhaps it was because you are more intelligent. Why are you more intelligent? Because you study more (which really means you are more righteous)? Or are you more intelligent because God gave you a gift of intelligence he withheld from others?

To be sure, most Christians who hold to the prevenient grace view would shrink from such answers. They see the implied arrogance in them. Rather they are more likely to say, "No, I chose Christ because I recognized my desperate need for him."

That certainly sounds more humble. But I must press the question. Why did you recognize your desperate need for Christ while your neighbor didn't? Was it because you were more righteous than your neighbor, or more intelligent?

The $64 question for advocates of prevenient grace is why some people cooperate with it and others don't. How we answer that will reveal how gracious we believe our salvation really is.

The $64,000 question is, "Does the Bible teach such a doctrine of prevenient grace? If so, where?"

We conclude that our salvation is of the Lord. He is the One who regenerates us. Those whom he regenerates come to Christ. Without regeneration no one will ever come to Christ. With regeneration no one will ever reject him. God's saving grace effects what he intends to effect by it (see John 6:37-40, 44).

SUMMARY OF CHAPTER 5

1. Our salvation flows from a divine initiative. It is God the Holy Spirit who sets the captives free. It is he who breathes into us spiritual life and resurrects us from spiritual death.

2. Our condition before we are quickened is one of spiritual death. It is more severe than mere mortal illness. There is not an ounce of spiritual life in us until God makes us alive.

3. Without rebirth no one will come to Christ. All who are reborn do come to Christ. Those who are dead to the things of God stay dead to the things of God unless God makes them alive. Those whom God makes alive, come alive. Salvation is of the Lord.

For Further Study

*And the LORD your God will circumcise your heart and the
heart of your descendants, to love the LORD your God with all
your heart and with all your soul, that you may live.*
(DEUTERONOMY 30:6)

*Because the palaces will be forsaken, the bustling city will be
deserted. The forts and towers will become lairs forever, a joy
of wild donkeys, a pasture of flocks—until the Spirit is poured
upon us from on high, and the wilderness becomes a fruitful
field, and the fruitful field is counted as a forest.*
(ISAIAH 32:14-15)

*Then He said to me, "Son of man, these bones are the whole
house of Israel. They indeed say, 'Our bones are dry, our hope
is lost, and we ourselves are cut off!' Therefore prophesy and
say to them, 'Thus says the Lord GOD: "Behold, O My people,
I will open your graves and cause you to come up from your
graves, and bring you into the land of Israel. Then you shall
know that I am the LORD, when I have opened your graves,
O My people, and brought you up from your graves. I will put
My Spirit in you, and you shall live, and I will place you in
your own land. Then you shall know that I, the LORD, have
spoken it and performed it," says the LORD.'"*
(EZEKIEL 37:11-14)

*Jesus answered and said to him, "Most assuredly, I say to you,
unless one is born again, he cannot see the kingdom of God."*
(JOHN 3:3)

*For the law of the Spirit of life in Christ Jesus has made me free
from the law of sin and death.* (ROMANS 8:2)

But God, who is rich in mercy, because of His great love with which He loved us, even when we were dead in trespasses, made us alive together with Christ (by grace you have been saved), and raised us up together, and made us sit together in the heavenly places in Christ Jesus, that in the ages to come He might show the exceeding riches of His grace in His kindness toward us in Christ Jesus. (EPHESIANS 2:4-7)

CHAPTER SIX

FOREKNOWLEDGE
AND
PREDESTINATION

The vast majority of Christians who reject the Reformed view of predestination adopt what is sometimes called the prescient or foreknowledge (pre-science, prior knowledge) view of predestination. Briefly stated, this view teaches that from all eternity God knew how we would live. He knew in advance whether we would receive Christ or reject Christ. He knew our free choices before we ever made them. God's choice of our eternal destiny then was made on the basis of what he knew we would choose. He chooses us because he knows in advance that we will choose him. The elect, then, are those who God knows will choose Christ freely.

In this understanding both the eternal decree of God and the free choice of man are left intact. In this view there is nothing arbitrary about God's decisions. There is no talk here of being reduced to puppets or of having our free wills violated. God is clearly absolved of any hint of wrongdoing. The basis for our ultimate judgment rests ultimately upon our decision for or against Christ.

There is much to commend this view of predestination. It is quite satisfying and has the benefits mentioned above. In addition it seems to have at least one strong biblical warrant. If we turn our attention again to Paul's letter to the Romans we read:

> For whom He foreknew, He also predestined to be conformed to the image of His Son, that He might be the firstborn among many brethren. Moreover whom He predestined, these He also called; whom He called, these He also justified; and whom He justified, these He also glorified. (Romans 8:29-30)

This well-known passage in Romans has been called the "Golden Chain of Salvation." We notice a kind of order here that begins with God's foreknowledge and is carried through to the glorification of the believer. It is crucial to the foreknowledge view that in this text God's foreknowledge comes *before* God's predestination.

I have great appreciation for the foreknowledge view of predestination. I once held it before I surrendered to the Reformed view. But I abandoned this view for several reasons. Not least is that I have become convinced that the foreknowledge view is not so much an explanation of the biblical doctrine of predestination as it is a denial of the biblical doctrine. It fails to include the whole counsel of God on the matter.

Perhaps the greatest weakness of the foreknowledge view is the text cited as its greatest strength. On closer analysis, the passage in Romans cited above becomes a serious problem for the foreknowledge view. On the one hand those who appeal to it to support the foreknowledge view find too little. That is, the passage teaches less than the advocates of foreknowledge would like it to teach and yet teaches more than they want it to teach.

How can this be? First, the conclusion that God's predestination is determined by God's foreknowledge is not taught by the passage. Paul does not come out and say that God chooses people on the basis of his prior knowledge of their choices. That idea is neither stated nor implied by the text. All the text declares is that God predestines those whom he foreknows. No one in this debate disputes that God has foreknowledge. Even God could not choose people he didn't know anything about. Before he could choose Jacob he had to have some idea in his mind of Jacob. But the text does not teach that God chose Jacob on the basis of Jacob's choice.

In fairness it must be said that at least the order of foreknowledge-predestination that we find in Romans 8 is compatible with the foreknowledge view. It is the rest of the passage that creates difficulty.

Note the order of events in the passage. Foreknowledge—predestination—calling—justification—glorification.

The crucial problem here has to do with the relationship of calling and justification. What does Paul mean here by "calling"? The New Testament speaks of divine calling in more than one way. In theology we distinguish between God's *external* call and God's *internal* call.

We find God's external call in the preaching of the gospel. When the gospel is preached, everyone who hears it is called or summoned to Christ. But not everyone responds positively. Not everyone who hears the outward call of the gospel becomes a believer. Sometimes the gospel call falls upon deaf ears.

Now we know that only those who respond to the outward call of the gospel in faith are justified. Justification is by faith. But again, not everyone whose ears hear the outward preaching of the gospel responds in faith. Therefore we must conclude that not all who are called outwardly are justified.

But Paul says in Romans that those whom God calls, he justifies. Now, we grant that the Bible does not explicitly say that all those he calls he justifies. We are supplying the word *all*. Perhaps we are as guilty of reading something into the text that is not there as those who advocate the foreknowledge view.

When we supply the word *all* here, we are responding to an implication of the text. We are making an inference. Is it a legitimate inference to make? I think it is.

If Paul does not mean that all who are called are justified, the only alternative would be that *some* who are called are justified. If we supply the word *some* instead of the word *all* here, then we must supply it throughout the Golden Chain. Then it would read like this:

> Some of those he foreknew, he also predestined. Some of those he predestined, he also called. Some of those he called, these he also justified. Some of those he justified, he also glorified.

This reading of the text leaves us with a theological monstrosity, a nightmare. It would mean that only some of the predestined ever hear the gospel and that only some of the justified are ultimately saved. These notions are utterly in conflict with what the rest of the Bible teaches on these matters.

Yet the foreknowledge view suffers an even bigger problem from the supplying of the word *some*. If God's predestination is based on his foreknowledge of how people will respond to the outward call of the gospel, how is it that only some of the predestined are even called? It would demand that God predestines some who are not called. If some of the predestined are predestined without being called, then God would not be basing his predestination on a prior knowledge of their response to his call. They could have no response to a call they never receive! God cannot have foreknowledge of a person's non-answer to a non-call.

Whew! If we follow all of that, then we will see the conclusion screaming at us. Paul cannot be implying the word *some*. Rather, the Golden Chain necessarily implies the word *all*.

Let's review the bidding. If we supply the word *some* to the Golden Chain the result is fatal to the foreknowledge view of predestination because it would have God predestinating some people who are not called. Since the view teaches that God's predestination is based upon God's foreknowledge of people's positive responses to the call of the gospel, then clearly the view collapses if some are predestined without a call.

The supplying of the word *all* is equally fatal to the foreknowledge view. This difficulty centers on the relationship of calling to justification. If all who are called are justified, then the passage could mean one of two things: *(A)* All who hear the gospel outwardly are justified; or *(B)* All who are called by God inwardly are justified.

If we answer with option *A*, then the conclusion we must reach is that everyone who ever hears the gospel is predestined to be saved. Of course the vast majority of those who hold the foreknowledge view of predestination also hold that not everyone who hears the gospel is saved. Some are universalists. They believe that everyone will be saved, whether or not they hear the gospel. But we must remember that the chief debate among evangelicals over predestination is not over the question of universalism. Both advocates of the Reformed view of predestination and advocates of the foreknowledge view agree that not everyone is saved. They agree that in fact there are people who hear the gospel outwardly (the external call of God) who do not respond in faith and who therefore are not justified. Option *A* is as repugnant to the advocates of the foreknowledge view as it is to the advocates of the Reformed view.

That leaves us with option *B:* All who are called inwardly by God are justified. What is the inward call of God? The outward call refers to the preaching of the gospel. Preaching is something that we do as human beings. The outward call can also be "heard" by reading the Bible. The Bible is the Word of God, but it comes to us in documents penned by human beings. In that sense it is external. No human being has the power to work inwardly on another human being. I cannot get inside a person's heart to work an immediate influence there. I can speak words that are outward. Those words may penetrate the heart, but I cannot make that happen by my own power. Only God can call a person inwardly. Only God can work immediately within the deepest chambers of the human heart to influence a positive response of faith.

So if option *B* is what the apostle means, then the implications are clear. If all whom God calls inwardly are justified and all whom God predestines are called inwardly, then it follows that God's foreknowledge concerns more than a mere prior awareness of the free decisions humans will make. To be sure, God does know from all eternity who will respond to the gospel and who will not. But such knowledge is not that of a mere passive observer. God knows from eternity whom he will inwardly call. All whom he inwardly calls he will also justify.

I said earlier that the Golden Chain teaches more than the foreknowledge view wants it to teach. It teaches that God predestines an inward call. All whom God predestines to be called inwardly will be justified. God is here doing something in the hearts of the elect to insure their positive response.

If option *B* is the correct understanding of the Golden Chain, then it is clear that God gives one kind of call to some people that he does not give to everyone. Since all who are called are justified and since not everyone is justified, then it follows that calling is a rather significant divine activity that some human beings receive and others do not.

Now we are forced back to a serious question not unlike our original question. Why is it that some are predestined to receive this call of God and others are not? Does the answer lie in man or in the purposes of God? An advocate of the foreknowledge view would have to answer that the reason God calls only some people inwardly is that he knows in advance who will respond positively to the inward call and who will not. Therefore he doesn't waste the inward call, he only gives it to those he knows will respond favorably to it.

How much power is there in God's inward call? Is there any advantage to receiving it? If it is only given to those who God knows will respond to it in their own power it would seem to be an inward influence without any *real* influence. If it does have any influence on the person who hears the outward call, then God is predestinating an advantage to some that he is withholding from others. If it has no influence on the human decision, then it is simply not an influence at all. If it is not an influence at all, then it is insignificant to salvation and a meaningless part of the Golden Chain.

It is crucial to remember that the inward call of God is given to people *before* they believe, *before* they respond in faith. If it influences the response in any way, then God is predestinating an advantage to the elect. If it does not influence the human decision, then what does it do? This dilemma is painful to the foreknowledge view, painful beyond relief.

The Reformed View of Predestination

In contrast with the foreknowledge view of predestination, the Reformed view asserts that the ultimate decision for salvation rests with God and not with man. It teaches that from all eternity God has chosen to intervene in the lives of some people and bring them to saving faith and has chosen not to do that for other people. From all eternity, without any prior view of our human behavior, God has chosen some unto election and others unto reprobation. The ultimate destiny of the individual is decided by God before that individual is even born and without depending ultimately upon the human choice. To be sure, a human choice is made, a free human choice, but the choice is made because God first chooses to influence the elect to make the right choice. The basis for God's choice does not rest in man but solely in the good pleasure of the divine will (see Romans 9:16).

In the Reformed view of predestination God's choice precedes man's choice. We choose him only because he has first chosen us. Without divine predestination and without the divine inward call, the Reformed view holds that nobody would ever choose Christ.

This is the view of predestination that rankles so many Christians. This is the view that raises serious questions about man's free will and about God's fairness. This is the view that provokes so many angry responses and charges of fatalism, determinism, and so on.

The Reformed view of predestination understands the Golden Chain as follows: From all eternity God foreknew his elect. He had an idea of their identities in his mind before he ever created them. He not only foreknew them in the sense of having a prior idea of their personal identities, but he also foreknew them in the sense of foreloving them. We must remember that when the Bible speaks of "knowing" it often distinguishes between a simple mental awareness of a person and a deep intimate love of the person.

The Reformed view believes that all whom God has thus foreknown he has also predestined to be inwardly called, to be justified, and to be glorified. God sovereignly brings to pass the salvation of his elect and only of his elect.

SUMMARY OF CHAPTER 6

1. Foreknowledge is not a valid explanation of predestination.
2. It makes redemption ultimately a human work.
3. Predestination is sidestepped and rendered virtually empty of significance.
4. The Golden Chain shows that our justification depends upon God's calling.
5. God's calling rests upon a prior predestination.
6. Without predestination there is no justification.
7. It is not our future choices, however, that induce God to choose us.
8. It is God's sovereign decision on our behalf.

For Further Study

> Then the word of the LORD came to me, saying: "Before
> I formed you in the womb I knew you; before you were
> born I sanctified you; I ordained you a prophet to the
> nations." (JEREMIAH 1:4-5)

> And when you pray, do not use vain repetitions as the
> heathen do. For they think that they will be heard for

their many words. Therefore do not be like them. For your Father knows the things you have need of before you ask Him. (MATTHEW 6:7-8)

Known to God from eternity are all His works. (ACTS 15:18)

And we know that all things work together for good to those who love God, to those who are the called according to His purpose. For whom He foreknew, He also predestined to be conformed to the image of His Son, that He might be the firstborn among many brethren. Moreover whom He predestined, these He also called; whom He called, these He also justified; and whom He justified, these He also glorified. (ROMANS 8:28-30)

Therefore do not be ashamed of the testimony of our Lord, nor of me His prisoner, but share with me in the sufferings for the gospel according to the power of God, who has saved us and called us with a holy calling, not according to our works, but according to His own purpose and grace which was given to us in Christ Jesus before time began. (2 TIMOTHY 1:8-9)

CHAPTER SEVEN

DOUBLE, DOUBLE, TOIL AND TROUBLE: IS PREDESTINATION DOUBLE?

Double predestination. The very words sound ominous. It is one thing to contemplate God's gracious plan of salvation for the elect. But what about those who are not elect? Are they also predestined? Is there a horrible decree of reprobation? Does God destine some unfortunate people to hell?

These questions immediately come to the fore as soon as double predestination is mentioned. Such questions make some declare the concept of double predestination out of bounds. Others, while believing in predestination, declare emphatically that they believe in *single* predestination. That is, while believing that some are predestined to salvation, there is no need to suppose that others are likewise predestined to damnation. In short, the idea is that some are predestined to salvation, but everyone has an opportunity to be saved. God makes sure that some make it by providing extra help, but the rest of mankind still has a chance.

Though there is strong sentiment to speak of single predestination only, and to avoid any discussion of double predestination, we must still face the questions on the table. Unless we conclude that every human being is predestined to salvation, we must face the flip side of election. If there is such a thing as predestination at all, and if that predestination does not include all people, then we must not shrink from the necessary inference that there are two sides to predestination. It is not enough to talk about Jacob; we must also consider Esau.

Equal Ultimacy

There are different views of double predestination. One of these is so frightening that many shun the term altogether, lest their view of the doctrine be confused with the scary one. This is called the equal ultimacy view.

Equal ultimacy is based on a concept of symmetry. It seeks a complete balance between election and reprobation. The key idea is this: Just as God intervenes in the lives of the elect to create faith in their hearts, so God equally intervenes in the lives of the reprobate to create or work unbelief in their hearts. The idea of God's actively working unbelief in the hearts of the reprobate is drawn from biblical statements about God hardening people's hearts.

Equal ultimacy is *not* the Reformed or Calvinist view of predestination. Some have called it "hyper-Calvinism." I prefer to call it "sub-Calvinism" or, better yet, "anti-Calvinism." Though Calvinism certainly has a view of double predestination, the double predestination it embraces is not one of equal ultimacy, which was condemned at the Second Council of Orange in 529.

To understand the Reformed view of the matter we must pay

close attention to the crucial distinction between *positive* and *negative* decrees of God. Positive has to do with God's active intervention in the hearts of the elect. Negative has to do with God's passing over the non-elect.

The Reformed view teaches that God positively or actively intervenes in the lives of the elect to insure their salvation. The rest of mankind God leaves to themselves. He does not create unbelief in their hearts. That unbelief is already there. He does not coerce them to sin. They sin by their own choices. In the Calvinist view the decree of election is positive; the decree of reprobation is negative.

Hyper-Calvinism's view of double predestination may be called *positive-positive predestination*. Orthodox Calvinism's view may be called *positive-negative predestination*. Let us view it in chart form:

CALVINISM	HYPER-CALVINISM
positive-negative	positive-positive
asymmetrical view	symmetrical view
unequal ultimacy	equal ultimacy
God passes over the	God works unbelief in the
reprobate.	hearts of the reprobate.

The dreadful error of hyper-Calvinism is that it involves God in coercing sin. This does radical violence to the integrity of God's character.

The primary biblical example that might tempt one toward hyper-Calvinism is the case of Pharaoh. Repeatedly we read in the Exodus account that God hardened Pharaoh's heart. God told Moses ahead of time that he would do this:

> You shall speak all that I command you. And Aaron
> your brother shall speak to Pharaoh, that he must send
> the children of Israel out of his land. And I will harden
> Pharaoh's heart, and multiply My signs and My wonders
> in the land of Egypt. But Pharaoh will not heed you, so
> that I may lay My hand on Egypt and bring My armies
> and My people, the children of Israel, out of the land of
> Egypt by great judgments. And the Egyptians shall know
> that I am the LORD, when I stretch out My hand on Egypt
> and bring out the children of Israel from among them.
> (Exodus 7:2-5)

The Bible clearly teaches that God did, in fact, harden Pharaoh's heart. Now we know that God did this for his own glory and as a sign to both Israel and Egypt. We know that God's purpose in all of this was a redemptive purpose. But we are still left with a nagging problem. God hardened Pharaoh's heart and then judged Pharaoh for his sin. How can God hold Pharaoh or anyone else accountable for sin that flows out of a heart that God himself hardened?

Our answer to that question will depend on how we understand God's act of hardening. How did he harden Pharaoh's heart? The Bible does not answer that question explicitly. As we think about it, we realize that basically there are only two ways he could have hardened Pharaoh's heart: actively or passively.

Active hardening would involve God's direct intervention within the inner chambers of Pharaoh's heart. God would intrude into Pharaoh's heart and create fresh evil in it. This would certainly insure that Pharaoh would bring forth the result that God was looking for. It would also insure that God is the author of sin.

Passive hardening is a totally different story. Passive hardening involves a divine judgment upon sin that is already present. All that God needs to do to harden the heart of a person whose heart is already desperately wicked is to "give him over to his sin." We find this concept of divine judgment repeatedly in Scripture.

How does this work? To understand it properly we must first look briefly at another concept, God's *common grace*. This refers to that grace of God that all men commonly enjoy. The rain that refreshes the earth and waters our crops falls upon the just and the unjust alike. The unjust certainly do not deserve such benefits, but they enjoy them anyway. So it is with sunshine and rainbows. Our world is a theater of common grace.

One of the most important elements of common grace we enjoy is the restraint of evil in the world. That restraint flows from many sources. Evil is restrained by policemen, laws, public opinion, balances of power, and so on. Though the world we live in is filled with wickedness, it is not as wicked as it possibly could be. God uses the means mentioned above as well as other means to keep evil in check. By his grace he controls and bridles the amount of evil in this world. If evil were left totally unchecked, then life on this planet would be impossible.

All that God has to do to harden people's hearts is to remove the restraints. He gives them a longer leash. Rather than restricting their human freedom, he increases it. He lets them have their own way. In a sense he gives them enough rope to hang themselves. It is not that God puts his hand on them to create fresh evil in their hearts; he merely removes his holy hand of restraint from them and lets them do their own will.

If we were to determine the most wicked, the most diabolical men of human history, certain names would appear on almost everyone's list. We would see the names of Hitler, Nero, Stalin, and others who have been guilty of mass murder and other atrocities. What do these people have in common? They were all dictators. They all had virtually unlimited power and authority within the sphere of their domains.

Why do we say that power corrupts and absolute power corrupts absolutely? (We know that this has no reference to God but only to the power and corruption of men.) Power corrupts precisely because it raises a person above the normal restraints that restrict the rest of us. I am restrained by conflicts of interest with people who are as powerful or more powerful than I am. We learn early in life to restrict our belligerence toward those who are bigger than we are. We tend to enter into conflicts selectively. Discretion tends to take over from valor when our opponents are more powerful than we.

Pharaoh was the most powerful man in the world when Moses went to see him. About the only restraint there was on Pharaoh's wickedness was the holy arm of God. All God had to do to harden Pharaoh further was to remove his arm. The evil inclinations of Pharaoh did the rest.

In the act of passive hardening, God makes a decision to remove the restraints; the wicked part of the process is done by Pharaoh himself. God does no violence to Pharaoh's will. As we said, he merely gives Pharaoh *more* freedom.

We see the same kind of thing in the case of Judas and with the wicked men whom God and Satan used to afflict Job. Judas was not a poor innocent victim of divine manipulation. He was not a righteous man whom God forced to betray Christ and then punished for the betrayal. Judas betrayed Christ because Judas wanted thirty pieces of silver. As the Scriptures declare, Judas was a son of perdition from the beginning.

To be sure, God uses the evil inclinations and evil intentions of fallen men to bring about his own redemptive purposes. Without Judas there is no Cross. Without the Cross there is no redemption. But this is not a case of God coercing evil. Rather it is a glorious case of God's redemptive triumph over evil. The evil desires of men's hearts cannot thwart God's sovereignty. Indeed they are subject to it.

When we study the pattern of God's punishment of wicked men we see a kind of poetic justice emerging. In the final judgment scene of the book of Revelation we read the following:

> He who is unjust, let him be unjust still; he who is filthy, let him be filthy still; he who is righteous, let him be righteous still; he who is holy, let him be holy still. (22:11)

In God's ultimate act of judgment he gives sinners over to their sins. In effect, he abandons them to their own desires. So it was with Pharaoh. By this act of judgment, God did not blemish his own righteousness by creating more evil in Pharaoh's heart. He established his own righteousness by punishing the evil that was already there in Pharaoh.

This is how we must understand double predestination. God gives mercy to the elect by working faith in their hearts. He gives justice to the reprobate by leaving them in their own sins. There is no symmetry here. One group receives mercy. The other group receives justice. No one is a victim of injustice. None can complain that there is unrighteousness in God.

Romans 9

The most significant passage in the New Testament that concerns double predestination is found in Romans 9.

For this is the word of promise: "At this time I will come and Sarah shall have a son." And not only this, but when Rebecca also had conceived by one man, even by our father Isaac (for the children not yet being born, nor having done any good or evil, that the purpose of God according to election might stand, not of works but of him who calls), it was said to her, "The older shall server the younger." As it is written, "Jacob I have loved, but Esau I have hated."

What shall we say then? Is there unrighteousness with God? Certainly not! For He says to Moses, "I will have mercy on whomever I will have mercy, and I will have compassion on whomever I will have compassion."

So then it is not of him who wills, nor of him who runs, but of God who shows mercy. For the Scripture says to Pharaoh, "Even for this same purpose I have raised you up, that I might show My power in you, and that My name might be declared in all the earth." Therefore He has mercy on whom He wills, and whom He wills He hardens. (vv. 9-18)

In this passage we have the clearest biblical expression we can find for the concept of double predestination. It is stated without reservation and without ambiguity: "Therefore He has mercy on whom He wills, and whom He wills He hardens." Some people get mercy, others get justice. The decision for this is in the hand of God.

Paul illustrates the double character of predestination by his reference to Jacob and Esau. These two men were twin brothers. They were carried in the same womb at the same time. One received the blessing of God and one did not. One received a special portion of the love of God, the other did not. Esau was "hated" by God.

The divine hatred mentioned here is not an expression of an insidious attitude of malice. It is what David earlier called a "holy hatred" (Psalm 139:22). Divine hatred is not malicious. It involves a withholding of favor. God is "for" those whom he loves. He turns his face against those wicked people who are not the objects of his special redemptive favor. Those whom he loves receive his mercy. Those whom he "hates" receive his justice. Again, no one is treated unjustly.

Why did God choose Jacob and not Esau? Some believe God must have foreseen something in Jacob that justified this special favor, that God looked down the corridors of time and saw Jacob making the right choice and Esau making the wrong choice. These people espouse the foreknowledge or prescient view of predestination, which we looked at in the previous chapter.

When I was converted to faith in Christ during my freshman year of college, I did not immediately become convinced of the doctrine of predestination. Although I realized the word *predestination* occurred frequently in the Bible, and that it was not an invention of Augustine, Martin Luther, or John Calvin, nevertheless I adopted the foreknowledge view, which is the most popular view of predestination among evangelicals. I doggedly held that view for several years, until, in my senior year of seminary, I took a course on the theology of Jonathan Edwards and was required to read his masterpiece *The Freedom of the Will*. It was Edwards's treatment of Paul's teaching on Romans 9 that finally caused me to surrender to the overwhelming clarity of the Word of God on this matter. I saw that Paul's teaching in Romans 9 not only demolishes the arguments of the opposition but dusts off the spot where they stood.

It must be said that the foreknowledge view and the Reformed view, as espoused by Edwards and others, agree as to the point in time when God elects people for salvation—eternity past. God's decree to save some individuals was made from all eternity, not last week, last year, or at some other point. However, the two views part ways when it comes to the basis for God's choice. As I noted above, the popular view is that he made his decree to save based on what he foresaw, but the Reformed view is that it was a sovereign decree of God without a view to anything he saw in the future. One view affirms the grace of God plus human actions, whereas the other affirms the grace of God alone.

When Paul wrote to the Romans, if he had been writing as an exponent of the foreknowledge view, it would not have been difficult to make the point clear. This was Paul's golden opportunity to teach a foreknowledge view of predestination. It seems strange indeed that he did not take such an opportunity. But this is no argument from silence. Paul does not remain mute on the subject. He labors the opposite point. He emphasizes the fact that God's decision was made before the birth of these twins, Jacob and Esau, and without a view to their future actions.

Paul's phrase in verse 11 is crucial: "For the children not yet being born, nor having done any good or evil, that the purpose of God according to election might stand, not of works but of Him who calls." Why does the apostle labor this point that the decree was not only made from all eternity, but was made before any one of these people had been born or had done anything good or evil?

Sometimes when we are interpreting a message or a document, we have to think through the authorial intent—that is, what the writer intended to convey. The quest for authorial intent can be dangerous, as it can lead interpreters to try to read the author's mind, so that they end up putting into the author's mouth words that were never there. However, when there are differences about the meaning of a passage after we have carefully looked at the words, it is appropriate to raise the question of authorial intent. Since evangelicals take different positions on the intent of Paul's words, I am raising the question here.

If Paul were teaching the foreknowledge view of predestination here, it would have made more sense for him to stop after saying that Jacob and Esau were predestined before they were born. By adding "nor having done any good or evil," Paul makes clear that divine predestination is based on God, not on us. The accent here is clearly on the work of God. Paul emphatically denies that election is a result of the work of man, foreseen or otherwise. It is the purpose of God according to his election that is in view.

But while Paul is silent about the question of future choices in verse 11, he does not remain so. In verse 16 he makes it clear: "So then it is not of him who wills, nor of him who runs, but of God who shows mercy." This is the *coup de grace* to Arminianism and all other non-Reformed views of predestination. This is the Word of God that requires all Christians to cease and desist from views of predestination that make the ultimate decision for salvation rest in the will of man. The apostle declares: "It is *not* of him who wills." The non-Reformed views must say that it *is* of him who wills. This is in violent contradiction to the teaching of Scripture. This one verse is absolutely fatal to Arminianism.

It is our duty to honor God. We must confess with the apostle that our election is not based on our wills but on the purposes of the will of God.

Anticipating Objections

One of the key techniques used in debate is anticipating the objections one's opponent will raise against one's position. If I am debating an issue, and I know my opponent cannot wait for me to stop talking so he can raise his objection, the most clever thing I can do is to raise it for him before he has the opportunity to raise it on his own. Whenever possible, I want to raise that objection as cogently as I possibly can. If possible, I want to make the objection more compelling than my opponent himself can. If I can do that, I have pulled the rug out from under my opponent's position.

I don't think anyone in Western thought was as adept at this technique as Paul the apostle, and we see that expertise on display here in Romans 9. Paul poses two rhetorical questions in this passage that counter objections his readers were likely to raise. The first is, "What shall we say then? Is there unrighteousness in God?" (v. 14). Paul was anticipating an objection along these lines: "What chance did Esau have to be elect if the choice was not his to make? It seems wrong of God to do it this way. God is unfair!"

Let's assume that Paul is teaching the foreknowledge view of predestination. If that is the case, why did he anticipate this objection? My Arminian friends have to defend their doctrine of predestination all the time. They are told that it is not true or not biblical. But I cannot imagine any Arminian ever having to defend his position against the charge that it isn't fair, that Arminianism somehow casts a shadow over the integrity of God and his righteousness. What could be more fair than that God would base his election unto salvation of one person over another on his knowledge of what they would do? If our election is ultimately based on human decisions, there is no need to raise such an objection.

It is to the biblical doctrine of predestination that this question is raised. It is predestination based on God's sovereign purpose, on his decision without a view to Jacob or Esau's choices, that prompts the outcry, "God is not fair!" But the outcry is based on a superficial understanding of the matter. It is the protest of fallen man complaining that God is not gracious enough.

How does Paul answer the question? He is not satisfied by merely saying, "No, there is no unrighteousness in God." Rather, his answer is as emphatic as he can make it. He says, "Certainly not!" or "God forbid!" depending on the translation you are reading.

Then Paul takes his readers to Scripture to back up his point. He writes, "For He says to Moses, 'I will have mercy on whomever I will have mercy, and I will have compassion on whomever I will have compassion'" (v. 15). In this citation from Exodus 33:19, God is simply declaring his sovereignty over his grace. He can pardon whom he will without being under any obligation to give the same mercy to another person. His grace is completely undeserved; indeed, there is nothing we can do to earn it. That leads to verse 16: "So then it is not of him who wills, nor of him who runs, but of God who shows mercy." As I noted earlier in the chapter, God does not treat everyone equally, but he cannot be charged with treating anyone unfairly. There is no unfairness with God.

The second objection Paul anticipates is this: "You will say to me then, 'Why does He still find fault? For who has resisted His will?'" (v. 19). Again we wonder why the apostle anticipates this objection. This is another objection never raised against Arminianism. Non-Reformed views of predestination don't have to worry about handling questions like this. God would obviously find fault with people who he knew would not choose Christ. If the ultimate basis for salvation rests in the power of human choice, then the blame is easily fixed and Paul would not have to wrestle with this anticipated objection. But he wrestles with it because the biblical doctrine of predestination demands that he wrestle with it.

How does Paul answer this question? Let us examine his reply:

> But indeed, O man, who are you to reply against God? Will the thing formed say to him who formed it, "Why have you made me like this?" Does not the potter have power over the clay, from the same lump to make one vessel for honor and the other for dishonor? What if God, wanting to show His wrath and to make His power known, endured with much longsuffering the vessels of wrath prepared for destruction, and that He might make known the riches of His glory on the vessels of mercy, which He had prepared beforehand for glory, even us whom He called, not of the Jews only, but also of the Gentiles? (Romans 9:20–24)

This is a heavy answer to the question. I must confess that I struggle with it. My struggle, however, is not over whether the passage teaches double predestination. It clearly does that. My struggle is with the fact that this text supplies ammunition for the advocates of equal ultimacy. It sounds like God is actively making people sinners. But that is not required by the text. He does make vessels of wrath and vessels of honor from the same lump of clay. But if we look closely at the text we will see that the clay with which the potter works is "fallen" clay. One batch of clay receives mercy in order to become vessels of honor. That mercy presupposes a clay that is already guilty. Likewise God must "endure" the vessels of wrath that are fit for destruction because they are guilty vessels of wrath.

Again the accent in this passage is on God's sovereign purpose and not upon man's free and good choices. The same assumptions are operating here that are operating in the first question.

The Arminian Reply

Some Arminians will reply to my treatment of this text with indignation. They agree that the passage teaches a strong view of divine sovereignty. Their objection will focus at another point. They will insist that Paul is not even talking about the predestination of individuals in Romans 9. Romans 9 is not about individuals but about God's electing of nations. Paul is here talking about Israel as God's chosen people. Jacob merely represents the nation Israel. His very name was changed to Israel and his sons became the fathers of the twelve tribes of Israel.

That God favored Israel over other nations is not in dispute. It was out of Israel that Jesus came. It was out of Israel that we received the Ten Commandments and the promises of the covenant with Abraham. We know that salvation is of the Jews.

That much is indeed true of Romans 9. We must consider, however, that in the electing of a nation God elected individuals. Nations are made up of individuals. Jacob was an individual. Esau was an individual. Here we see clearly that God sovereignly elected individuals as well as a nation. We must hasten to add that Paul *extends* this treatment of election beyond Israel in verse 24 when he declares: "even us whom He called, not of the Jews only, but also of the Gentiles."

Unconditional Election

Let us return for a moment to our famous acrostic, TULIP. We have already quarreled with the *T* and the *I* and changed it to

RULEP. Though I prefer the term *sovereign election* to *unconditional election*, I will not damage the acrostic further. If we changed it to RSLEP it wouldn't even rhyme with TULIP.

Unconditional election means that our election is decided by God according to his purpose, according to his sovereign will. It is not based upon some foreseen condition that some of us meet and others fail to meet. It is not based on our willing or on our running, but upon the sovereign purpose of God.

The term *unconditional election* can be misleading and grossly abused. I once met a man who never darkened the door of a church and who showed no evidence of being a Christian. He made no profession of faith and was engaged in no Christian activity. He told me that he believed in unconditional election. He was confident that he was elect. He did not have to trust Christ, he did not have to repent, he did not have to be obedient to Christ. He declared that he was elect and that was enough. No further conditions for salvation were necessary for him. He was, in his opinion, saved, sanctified, and satisfied.

We must be careful to distinguish between conditions that are necessary for salvation and conditions that are necessary for election. We often speak of election and salvation as if they were synonymous, but they are not exactly the same thing. Election is *unto* salvation. Salvation in its fullest sense is the complete work of redemption that God accomplishes in us.

There are all sorts of conditions that must be met for someone to be saved. Chief among them is that we must have faith in Christ. Justification is by faith. Faith is a necessary requirement. To be sure, the Reformed doctrine of predestination teaches that all the elect are indeed brought to faith. God insures that the conditions necessary for salvation are met.

When we say that election is unconditional we mean that the

original decree of God by which he chooses some people to be saved is not dependent upon some future condition in us that God foresees. There is nothing in us that God could foresee that would induce him to choose us. The only thing he would foresee in the lives of fallen creatures left to themselves would be sin. God chooses us simply according to the good pleasure of his will (see Ephesians 1:5).

Is God Arbitrary?

That God chooses us not because of what he finds in us, but according to his own good pleasure, gives rise to the charge that this makes God arbitrary. It suggests that God makes his selection in a whimsical or capricious manner. It seems like our election is the result of a blind and frivolous lottery. If we are elect, then it is only because we are lucky. God pulled our names out of a celestial hat.

To be arbitrary is to do something for no reason. Now, it is clear that there is no reason found *in us* for God to choose us. But that is not the same as saying that God has no reason in himself. God doesn't do anything without a reason. He is not capricious or whimsical. God is as sober as he is sovereign.

A lottery is intentionally left up to chance. God does not operate by chance. He knew whom he would select. He foreknew—that is, foreloved—his elect. It was not a blind draw because God is not blind. Yet we still must insist that it was nothing that he foreknew, foresaw, or foreloved in us that was the decisive reason for his choice.

Calvinists do not generally like to speak of luck. Instead of wishing people "good luck," we might say, "Providential blessings." Yet if we were to speak of our "lucky day," we would mark that day in eternity when God decided to choose us.

Let us turn our attention to Paul's teaching on this matter in Ephesians:

> Blessed be the God and Father of our Lord Jesus Christ, who has blessed us with every spiritual blessing in the heavenly places in Christ, just as He chose us in Him before the foundation of the world, that we should be holy and without blame before Him in love, having predestined us to adoption as sons by Jesus Christ to Himself, according to the good pleasure of His will, to the praise of the glory of His grace, by which He has made us accepted in the Beloved. (1:3-6)

"According to the good pleasure of his will." This is the apostolic statement that seems to suggest divine arbitrariness. The chief culprit is the word *pleasure*. In our vocabulary the word *pleasure* is often charged with the meaning of wild, reckless abandon. Pleasure is that which feels good, something that has sensual and emotional overtones. We are aware of vices that bring wicked pleasure to us.

When the Bible speaks of God's pleasure, the term is not used in such a frivolous manner. Here pleasure means simply "that which is pleasing." God predestines us according to what pleases him. The Bible speaks of God's *good* pleasure. God's good pleasure must never be mistaken for an evil pleasure. What pleases God is goodness. What pleases us is not always goodness. God never takes pleasure in wickedness. There is nothing wicked about the good pleasure of his will. Though the reason for choosing us does not lie in us but in the sovereign divine pleasure, we may rest assured that the sovereign divine pleasure is a good pleasure.

We remember also what the apostle instructed the Philippian Christians. He said to them: "Work out your own salvation with fear and trembling; for it is God who works in you both to will and to do for His good pleasure" (Philippians 2:12-13).

In this passage Paul is not teaching that election is a joint enterprise between God and man. Election is exclusively the work of God. It is, as we have seen, *monergistic*. Paul is speaking here about the outworking of our salvation that follows our election. He is specifically referring here to the process of our sanctification. Sanctification is not monergistic. It is *synergistic*. That is, it demands the cooperation of the regenerate believer. We are called to work to grow in grace. We are to work hard, resisting sin unto blood if necessary, pummeling our bodies if that is what it takes to subdue them.

We are called to this sober work of sanctification by a divine summons. The work is to be carried out in a spirit of fear and trembling. Our sanctification is not a casual matter. We do not approach it in a cavalier manner, saying simply, "Let go and let God." God does not do it all for us.

Neither, however, does God leave us to work out our own salvation by ourselves, in our own strength. We are comforted by his sure promise to be working in us both to do and to will what is pleasing him.

I once heard a sermon by the great Scottish preacher Eric Alexander in which he stressed that God is working in us for *his* good pleasure. Paul does not say that God is working in us for *our* good pleasure. We are not always entirely pleased by what God is doing in our lives. Sometimes we experience a conflict between the purpose of God and our own purpose. I never choose to suffer on purpose. Yet it may well be within the sovereign purpose of God that I suffer. He promises us that by his sovereignty all things work together for good for those who love him and are called according to his purpose (see Romans 8:28).

My purposes do not always include God's good. I am a sinner. Fortunately for us, God is not a sinner. He is altogether righteous (see Psalm 89:14). His purposes are always and everywhere righteous. His purposes work for my good, even when his purposes are in conflict with my purposes. Perhaps I should say, *especially* when his purposes are in conflict with my purposes. What pleases him is good for me. That is one of the most difficult lessons Christians ever learn.

Our election is unconditional except for one thing. There is one requirement we must meet before God will ever elect us. To be elect we must first be sinners.

God does not elect righteous people unto salvation. He does not need to elect righteous people unto salvation. Righteous people do not need to be saved. Only sinful people are in need of a savior. Those who are well have no need of a physician.

Christ came to seek and to save people who were really lost. God sent him into the world not only to make our salvation possible, but to make it sure. Christ has not died in vain. His sheep are saved through his sinless life and his atoning death. There is nothing arbitrary about that.

SUMMARY OF CHAPTER 7

1. Not all men are predestined to salvation.
2. There are two aspects or sides to the question. There are those who are elect and those who are not elect.
3. Predestination is "double."
4. We must be careful not to think in terms of equal ultimacy.
5. God does not create sin in the hearts of sinners.
6. The elect receive mercy. The non-elect receive justice.

7. No one receives injustice at the hands of God.
8. God's "hardening of hearts" is itself a just punishment for sin that is already present.
9. God's choice of the elect is sovereign, not arbitrary or capricious.
10. All of God's decisions flow from his holy character.

For Further Study

> For you are a people holy to the LORD your God. The LORD your God has chosen you to be a people for his treasured possession, out of all the peoples who are on the face of the earth. It was not because you were more in number than any other people that the Lord set his love on you and chose you, for you were the fewest of all peoples, but it is because the LORD loves you and is keeping the oath that he swore to your fathers, that the LORD has brought you out with a mighty hand and redeemed you from the house of slavery, from the hand of Pharaoh king of Egypt. (DEUTERONOMY 7:6-8, ESV)

> And the LORD said to her: "Two nations are in your womb, two peoples shall be separated from your body; one people shall be stronger than the other, and the older shall serve the younger." (GENESIS 25:23)

> And the LORD said to Moses, "When you go back to Egypt, see that you do all those wonders before Pharaoh which I have put in your hand. But I will harden his heart, so that he will not let the people go." (EXODUS 4:21)

> "I have loved you," says the LORD. "Yet you say, 'In what way have You loved us?' Was not Esau Jacob's brother?" says the LORD. "Yet Jacob I have loved; but Esau I have hated." (MALACHI 1:2-3)

Now when the Gentiles heard this, they were glad and glorified the word of the Lord. And as many as had been appointed to eternal life believed. (ACTS 13:48)

And not only this, but when Rebecca also had conceived by one man, even by our father Isaac (for the children not yet being born, nor having done any good or evil, that the purpose of God according to election might stand, not of works but of Him who calls), it was said to her, "The older shall serve the younger." As it is written, "Jacob I have loved, but Esau I have hated." (ROMANS 9:10-13)

They stumble, being disobedient to the word, to which they also were appointed. (1 PETER 2:8)

CHAPTER EIGHT

CAN WE KNOW THAT WE ARE SAVED?

The ministry of Evangelism Explosion keys its presentation of the gospel upon two crucial questions. The first is, "Have you come to the place in your spiritual life where you know *for sure* that when you die you will go to heaven?" Experienced workers say the vast majority of people answer this question in the negative. Most people are not sure of their future salvation. Many, if not most, raise serious doubts about whether such assurance is even possible.

When I was in seminary, a poll was taken of my classmates. Of that particular group of seminarians approximately 90 percent said that they were not sure of their salvation. Many expressed anger at the question, seeing in it a kind of implied presumptuousness. It seems arrogant to some people even to talk about assurance of salvation.

To be sure, stating our assurance of salvation may be an act of arrogance. If our confidence in our salvation rests in a confidence in ourselves, it is an act of arrogance. If we are sure we are going to heaven because we think we deserve to go to heaven, then it is unspeakably arrogant.

With respect to the assurance of salvation there are basically four kinds of people in the world. (1) There are people who are not saved who know that they are not saved. (2) There are people who are saved who do not know that they are saved. (3) There are people who are saved who know that they are saved. (4) There are people who are not saved who "know" that they are saved.

It is the last group that throws a monkey wrench into the works. If there are people who are *not* saved who "know" that they are saved, how can the people who *are* saved know that they really are saved?

To answer that question we must first ask another question. Why do some people have a false assurance of their salvation? Actually it is relatively easy. False assurance stems chiefly from false understanding of what salvation requires or entails.

Suppose, for example, that a person is a universalist. He believes that everybody is saved. If that premise is correct, then the rest of his logical deduction is easy. His reasoning goes like this:

Everybody is saved.
I am a body.
Therefore, I am saved.

Universalism is far more prevalent than many of us realize. When my son was five years old I asked him the two questions from Evangelism Explosion. He answered the first question in the affirmative. He was sure that when he died he would go to heaven. I proceeded then to the second question. "If you were to die tonight and God said to you, 'Why should I let you into my heaven?' what would you answer?" My son did not hesitate. He answered immediately, "Because I'm dead!"

By the time my son was five years old he already had received a message loud and clear. The message was that everyone who dies goes to heaven. His doctrine of justification was not justification by faith alone. It was not even justification by works, or a combination of faith and works. His doctrine was much simpler; he believed in justification by death. He had a false assurance of his salvation.

If universalism is widespread in our culture, so is the concept of justification by works. In a statistical survey of over a thousand people who were asked the same question I asked my son, over 80 percent of them gave an answer that involved some sort of "works righteousness." People said things like, "I have gone to church for thirty years"; "I have perfect attendance in Sunday school"; or "I have never done any serious harm to anybody."

I learned one thing clearly in my experience in Evangelism Explosion: The message of justification by faith alone has not penetrated our culture. Multitudes of people are resting their hopes for heaven on their own good works. They are quite willing to admit that they are not perfect, but they assume that they are good enough. They have done their "best" and that, they tragically assume, is good enough for God.

I remember a student protesting to John Gerstner about a grade he received on a term paper. He punctuated his complaint by saying, "Dr. Gerstner, I did my best." Gerstner looked at him and said softly, "Young man, you have *never* done your best."

Surely we do not believe that we have done our best. If we review our performance for the last twenty-four hours we will know that we have not done our best. It is not necessary to review our entire lives to see how specious such a statement is.

Yet even if we granted what we never in fact would grant, that people do their best, we know that even that is not good enough. God requires perfection to get into his heaven. We either find that perfection in ourselves or we find it somewhere else, in someone else. If we think we can find it in ourselves, we delude ourselves and the truth is not in us (see 1 John 1:8).

We see then that it is quite easy to have a false sense of security about our salvation. But what if we do have a proper understanding of what salvation requires, does that guarantee that we will avoid a false assurance of salvation?

By no means. The devil himself knows what is required for salvation. He knows who the Savior is. He understands the intellectual part of salvation better than we do. But he does not put his personal trust in Christ for his salvation. He hates the Jesus who is the Savior.

We can have a proper understanding of what salvation is and still delude ourselves about whether or not we meet the requirements of salvation. We may think that we have faith when in fact we have no faith. We may think that we are believing in Christ but the Christ we embrace is not the biblical Christ. We may think that we love God but the God we love is an idol.

Do we love a God who is sovereign? Do we love a God who sends people to hell? Do we love a God who demands absolute obedience? Do we love a Christ who will say to some on the last day, "Depart from me, I never knew you"? I am not asking whether we love this God and this Christ perfectly; I am asking whether we love this God and this Christ at all.

One of my all-time favorite anecdotes was told by Dr. James Montgomery Boice. Dr. Boice spoke of a mountain climber who slipped from his moorings and was about to plunge thousands of feet to his death. In panic he grabbed a scrawny bush that was growing out of a rock on the side of the mountain. It momentarily broke his fall, but it was slowly coming out of its place by the roots. The climber looked to heaven and cried, "Is there anybody up there who can help me?" A deep bass voice was heard

from the sky. "Yes, I will help you. Trust me. Let go of the bush."
The climber looked into the cavern below and cried once more,
"Is there anyone *else* up there who can help me?"

It is possible that the God we believe in is "someone else." I have
often spoken to staff persons associated with Young Life, the ministry that has an outstanding mission to teenagers. The strength
of Young Life is at the same time its greatest danger. Young Life
has a frighteningly high rate of youngsters who make professions
of faith and later repudiate that profession.

Young Life has done an outstanding job of relating to teenagers. They are masters at making the gospel attractive. The
danger is, however, that Young Life is so attractive, so neat, that
young people can be converted to Young Life and never deal with
the biblical Christ. That in no way is intended as a criticism of
Young Life. I am not suggesting that we should therefore seek to
make the gospel unattractive. We do enough of that already. It is
only to point out what we all must be reminded of, that people
can respond to us, or to our group, as a substitute for Christ, and
thereby gain a false assurance of salvation.

From a biblical standpoint we must realize that it is still not
only possible for us to have a genuine assurance of our salvation,
but that it is our *duty* to seek such assurance. If assurance is possible and if it is commanded, it is not arrogant to seek it. It is
arrogant not to seek it.

The apostle Peter writes:

> Therefore, brethren, be even more diligent to make your
> calling and election sure, for if you do these things you
> will never stumble; for so an entrance will be supplied to
> you abundantly into the everlasting kingdom of our Lord
> and Savior Jesus Christ. (2 Peter 1:10-11)

Here we see the mandate to make our election sure. To do so requires diligence. We have a pastoral concern here. Peter links assurance with freedom from stumbling. One of the most important factors that contribute to a Christian's spiritual growth, a consistent spiritual growth, is the assurance of salvation. There are many Christians who are indeed in a state of salvation who lack assurance. To be lacking in assurance is a grave hindrance to spiritual growth. The person who is not sure of his state of grace is exposed to doubts and terrors in his soul. He lacks an anchor for his spiritual life. His uncertainty makes him tentative in his walk with Christ.

Not only is it important that we gain authentic assurance but it is important that we gain it early in our Christian experience. It is a key element in our growth toward maturity. Pastors need to be aware of that and assist their flocks in the diligent search for assurance.

I never know for sure whether another person I meet is elect or not. I cannot see into other people's hearts. As human beings our view of others is restricted to outward appearances. The only person who can know for sure that you are elect is you.

Who can know for sure that he is not elect? Nobody. You may be certain that at this moment you are not in a state of grace. You cannot know for certain that tomorrow you will not be in a state of grace. There are multitudes of elect people walking around who are as yet unconverted.

Such a person might say, "I don't know if I am elect or not and I am not the least bit concerned about it." There can hardly be any greater folly. If you do not yet know if you are elect, I can think of no more urgent question to answer.

If you are not sure, you would be well advised to make sure.

Don't ever assume that you are not elect. Make your election a matter of certainty.

The apostle Paul was sure of his election. He frequently used the term *we* when he spoke of the elect. He said toward the end of his life:

> For I am already being poured out as a drink offering, and the time of my departure is at hand. I have fought the good fight, I have finished the race, I have kept the faith. Finally, there is laid up for me the crown of righteousness, which the Lord, the righteous Judge, will give to me on that Day, and not to me only but also to all who have loved His appearing. (2 Timothy 4:6-8)

Earlier in the same epistle he declared:

> For this reason I also suffer these things; nevertheless I am not ashamed, for I know whom I have believed and am persuaded that He is able to keep what I have committed to Him until that Day. (1:12)

How can we, like Paul, have true assurance, assurance that is not spurious? True assurance is grounded in the promises of God for our salvation. Our assurance comes first of all from our trust in the God who makes these promises. Secondly, our assurance is enhanced by the *inward evidence* of our own faith. We know that we could never have any true affection for Christ if we were not reborn. We know that we could not be reborn if we were not elect. A knowledge of sound theology is vital to our assurance. If we have a correct understanding of election, that understanding will help us interpret these inward evidences.

I know inwardly that I do not love Christ totally. But at the same time I do know that I love him. I rejoice inwardly at the thought of his triumph. I rejoice inwardly at the thought of his coming. I will rejoice at his exaltation. I know that none of these sentiments that I find in myself could possibly be there if it were not for grace.

When a man and woman are in love we assume that they are aware of it. A person is usually able to discern whether or not he or she is in love with another person. This comes from an inward assurance.

In addition to the inward evidence of grace there is also outward evidence. We should be able to see visible fruit of our conversion. The outward evidence, however, may also cause our lack of assurance. We can see the abiding sin in our lives. Such sin does not do much for our assurance. We see ourselves sinning and we ask ourselves, "How can I do these things if I really love Christ?"

To have assurance we must make a sober analysis of our lives (see 2 Corinthians 13:5). It is not much use to compare ourselves with others. We will always be able to find others who are more advanced in their sanctification than we are. We may also be able to find others who are less advanced. No two people are ever at exactly the same point in their spiritual growth.

We must ask ourselves if we see any real change in our behavior, any real outward evidence of grace. This is a precarious process because we can lie to ourselves. It is a difficult task to perform, but by no means impossible.

We have one more vital method of reaching assurance. We are told in Scripture about the internal witness of the Holy Spirit. Paul states that "the Spirit Himself bears witness with our spirit that we are children of God" (Romans 8:16).

The chief means by which the Spirit testifies to us is through his Word. I never have greater assurance than when I am meditating on the Word of God. If we neglect this means of grace, it is difficult to have any lasting or strong assurance of our salvation.

One Reformed theologian, A. A. Hodge, gives the following list of distinctions between true assurance and false assurance:

TRUE ASSURANCE	FALSE ASSURANCE
begets unfeigned humility	begets spiritual pride
leads to diligence in holiness	leads to slothful indulgence
leads to honest self-examination	avoids accurate evaluation
leads to desire for more intimate fellowship with God	is cold toward fellowship with God

Assurance of salvation can be augmented or diminished. We can increase our assurance or we can decrease it. We can even lose it altogether, at least for a season. There are many things that can cause our assurance to slip away from us. We can grow negligent in our preserving of it. The diligence to which we are called to make our election sure is an ongoing diligence. If we become smug in our assurance and begin to take it for granted, we run the risk of losing that assurance.

The greatest peril to our continued assurance is a fall into some serious and gross sin. We know the love that covers a multitude of sins. We know that we do not have to be perfect to have assurance of salvation. But when we fall into special sorts of sins, our assurance is shaken brutally. David's sin of adultery caused him to tremble in terror before God. If we read his prayer of confession in Psalm 51 we can hear the lament of a man who is struggling to regain his assurance. After Peter cursed and denied Christ and Christ's eyes fell upon him, what was the state of Peter's assurance?

We all experience periods of spiritual coldness in which we feel as though God has totally removed the light of his countenance from us. The saints have called it the "dark night of the soul." There are times when we feel as though God has abandoned us. We think that he no longer hears our prayers. We do not feel the sweetness of his presence. At times like these, when our assurance is at a low ebb, we must incline ourselves toward him with all of our might. He promises us that, if we will draw near to him, he in turn will come near to us (see James 4:8).

Finally, we may be shaken in our assurance if we are exposed to great suffering. A serious illness, a painful accident, a loss of a loved one to death may disturb our assurance. We know that Job cried out, "Though He slay me, yet will I trust him." That was the cry of a man in pain. He said that he was sure that his Redeemer lived, but I am certain that Job had his moments when doubts assailed him.

Again it is the Word of God that comforts us in times of trial. Our tribulations have the ultimate effect not of destroying our hope but of establishing it. Peter wrote:

> Beloved, do not think it strange concerning the fiery
> trial which is to try you, as though some strange thing
> happened to you; but rejoice to the extent that you partake
> of Christ's sufferings, that when His glory is revealed, you
> may also be glad with exceeding joy. (1 Peter 4:12-13)

When we are attentive to the promises of God, our suffering may be used to increase our assurance rather than diminish it. We need not have a crisis of faith. Our faith may be strengthened through suffering. God promises that our suffering will not merely result ultimately in joy, but in *exceeding* joy.

Can We Lose Our Salvation?

We have already stated that it is possible to lose our assurance of salvation. That does not mean, however, that we can lose salvation itself. We are moving now to the question of eternal security. Can a justified person lose his justification?

We know how the Roman Catholic Church has answered that question. Rome insists that the grace of justification can in fact be lost. The sacrament of Penance, which demands Confession, was established for this very reason. Rome calls the sacrament of Penance the "second plank of justification for those who have made shipwreck of their souls."

According to Rome, saving grace is destroyed in the soul when a person commits a "mortal" sin. Mortal sin is so called because it has the power to kill grace. Grace can die. If it is destroyed by mortal sin, it must be restored through the sacrament of penance, or the sinner himself finally perishes.

The Reformed do not believe in mortal sin in the way Rome does. We believe that all sins are mortal in the sense that they deserve death but that no sin is mortal in the sense that it destroys the grace of salvation in the elect. (Later, we will consider the "unpardonable sin" about which Jesus warned.)

The Reformed view of eternal security is called the "perseverance of the saints," the *P* in TULIP. The idea here is, "Once in grace, always in grace." Another way of stating it is, "If you have it, you never lose it; if you lose it, you never had it."

Our confidence in the perseverance of the saints does not rest upon our confidence in the saints' ability, in themselves, to persevere. Again, I would like to modify the acrostic TULIP slightly. Same letter, new word. I prefer to speak of the *preservation* of the saints.

The reason true Christians do not fall from grace is that God graciously keeps them from falling. Perseverance is what we do. Preservation is what God does. We persevere because God preserves.

The doctrine of eternal security or perseverance is based on the promises of God. A few of the key biblical passages are listed below:

> Being confident of this very thing, that He who has begun a good work in you will complete it until the day of Jesus Christ. (Philippians 1:6)

> My sheep hear My voice, and I know them, and they follow Me. And I give them eternal life, and they shall never perish; neither shall anyone snatch them out of My hand. My Father, who has given them to Me, is greater than all; and no one is able to snatch them out of My Father's hand. (John 10:27-29)

> Blessed be the God and Father of our Lord Jesus Christ, who according to His abundant mercy has begotten us again to a living hope through the resurrection of Jesus Christ from the dead, to an inheritance incorruptible and undefiled and that does not fade away, reserved in heaven

for you, who are kept by the power of God through
faith for salvation ready to be revealed in the last time.
(1 Peter 1:3-5)

For by one offering He has perfected forever those who are
being sanctified. (Hebrews 10:14)

Who shall bring a charge against God's elect? It is God
who justifies. Who is he who condemns? It is Christ
who died, and furthermore is also risen, who is even
at the right hand of God, who also makes intercession
for us. Who shall separate us from the love of Christ?
Shall tribulation, or distress, or persecution, or famine,
or nakedness, or peril, or sword? As it is written: "For
Your sake we are killed all day long; we are accounted
as sheep for the slaughter." Yet in all these things we are
more than conquerors through Him who loved us. For
I am persuaded that neither death nor life, nor angels nor
principalities nor powers, nor things present nor things to
come, nor height nor depth, nor any other created thing,
shall be able to separate us from the love of God which is
in Christ Jesus our Lord. (Romans 8:33-39)

We see from these passages that the ground for our confidence
in perseverance is the power of God. God promises to finish what
he starts. Our confidence does not rest in the will of man. This
difference between the will of man and the power of God sepa-
rates Calvinists from Arminians. The Arminian holds that God
elects persons to eternal life only on the condition of their voluntary cooperation with grace and perseverance in grace until death,
as foreseen by him.

The Roman Catholic church, for example, has decreed the following: "If anyone says that a man once justified cannot lose grace and therefore that he who falls and sins never was truly justified, let him be accursed" (Council of Trent: 6/23).

Protestant Arminians made a similar statement: "Persons truly regenerate, by neglecting grace and grieving the Holy Spirit with sin, fall away totally, and at length finally, from grace into eternal reprobation" (*see* Conference of Remonstrants 11/7).

A chief argument given by Arminians is that it is inconsistent with man's free will for God to "force" his perseverance. Yet the Arminians themselves believe that believers will not fall from grace in heaven. In our glorified state God will render us incapable of sinning. Yet the glorified saints in heaven are still free. If preservation and free will are consistent conditions in heaven, they cannot possibly be inconsistent conditions here on earth. The Arminians again try to prove too much with their view of human freedom. If God can preserve us in heaven without destroying our free will, he can preserve us on earth without destroying our free will.

We are able to persevere only because God works within us, with our free wills. And because God is at work in us, we are certain to persevere. The decrees of God concerning election are immutable. They do not change, because he does not change. All whom he justifies he glorifies. None of the elect is ever lost.

Why, then, does it seem to us that many people do fall away from grace? We have all known people who made zealous starts with the Christian faith only to repudiate their faith later. We have heard of great Christian leaders who have committed gross sins and scandalized their profession of faith.

Reformed theology readily acknowledges that people make professions of faith and then repudiate them. We know that

Christians "backslide." We know that Christians are capable of and do in fact commit gross and heinous sins.

We believe that true Christians can fall seriously and radically. We do not believe that they can fall *totally* and *finally*. We observe the case of King David, who was guilty not only of adultery but of conspiracy in the death of Uriah, Bathsheba's husband. David used his power and authority to make sure Uriah was killed in battle. In essence David was guilty of murder in the first degree, premeditated and with malice aforethought.

David's conscience was so seared, his heart so hardened, that it required nothing less than direct confrontation with a prophet of God to bring him to his senses. His subsequent repentance was as deep as his sin. David sinned radically but not totally and finally. He was restored.

Consider the record of two famous persons in the New Testament. Both of them were called by Jesus to be disciples. Both of them walked beside Jesus during his earthly ministry. Both of them betrayed Jesus. Their names are Peter and Judas.

After Judas betrayed Christ, he went out and committed suicide. After Peter betrayed Christ, he repented and was restored, emerging as a pillar of the early church. What was the difference between these two men? Jesus predicted that both of them would betray him. When he finished speaking with Judas, he said to him, "What you have to do, do quickly."

Jesus spoke differently to Peter. He said to him: "Simon, Simon! Indeed, Satan has asked for you, that he may sift you as wheat. But I have prayed for you, that your faith should not fail; and when you have returned to Me, strengthen your brethren" (Luke 22:31-32).

Notice carefully what Jesus said. He did not say *if* but *when*.

Jesus was confident that Peter would return. His fall would be radical and serious, but not total and final.

It is clear that Jesus' confidence in Peter's return was not based on Peter's strength. Jesus knew that Satan would sift Peter like wheat. That is like saying that Peter was a "piece of cake," "duck soup," for Satan. Jesus' confidence was based upon the power of Jesus' intercession. It is from the promise of Christ that he would be our Great High Priest, our Advocate with the Father, our Righteous Intercessor, that we believe that we will persevere. Our confidence is in our Savior and our Priest who prays for us.

The Bible records a prayer that Jesus offered for us in John 17. We ought to read this great High Priestly Prayer frequently. Let us examine a portion of it:

> . . . keep through Your name those whom You have given Me, that they may be one as We are. While I was with them in the world, I kept them in Your name. Those whom You gave Me I have kept; and none of them is lost except the son of perdition, that the Scripture might be fulfilled. (vv. 11-12)

Again we read:

> Father, I desire that they also whom You gave Me may be with Me where I am, that they may behold My glory which You have given Me; for You loved Me before the foundation of the world. (v. 24)

Our preservation is a Trinitarian work. God the Father keeps and preserves us. God the Son intercedes for us. God the Holy Spirit indwells and assists us. We are given the "seal" and the "earnest" of the Holy Spirit (see 2 Timothy 2:19; Ephesians 1:14; Romans 8:23). These images are all images of a divine guarantee. The seal of the Spirit is an indelible mark like the waxed imprint of a monarch's signet ring. It indicates that we are his possession. The earnest of the Spirit is not identical to earnest money that is paid in modern real estate transactions. Such earnest money may be forfeited. In biblical terms the earnest of the Spirit is a down payment with a promise to pay the rest. God does not forfeit his earnest. He does not fail to finish the payments he began. The first fruits of the Spirit guarantee that the last fruits will be forthcoming.

An analogy of God's work of preservation may be seen in the image of a father holding onto his small child's hand as they walk together. In the Arminian view the safety of the child rests in the strength of the child's grip on the father's hand. If the child lets go he will perish. In the Calvinist view the safety of the child rests in the strength of the father's grip on the child. If the child's grip fails, the father's grip holds firm. The arm of the Lord does not wax short.

Still we ask why it seems that some people do in fact fall away totally and finally. Here we must echo the words of the apostle John: "They went out from us, but they were not of us; for if they had been of us, they would have continued with us; but they went out that they might be made manifest, that none of them were of us" (1 John 2:19).

We repeat our aphorism: If we have it we never lose it; if we lose it we never had it. We recognize that the church of Jesus Christ is a mixed body. There are tares that live side by side with the wheat; goats that live side by side with sheep. The parable of the sower makes it plain that people can experience a false conversion. They may have an appearance of faith, but that faith may not be genuine.

We know people who have been "converted" many times. Every time there is a church revival they go to the altar and get "saved." One minister told of a man in his congregation who had been "saved" seventeen times. During a revival meeting the evangelist made an altar call for all who wanted to be filled with the Spirit. The man who had been converted so often made his way toward the altar again. A woman from the congregation shouted, "Don't fill him, Lord. He leaks!"

We all leak to some degree, but no Christian is totally and finally bereft of God's Spirit. Those who become "unconverted" were never converted in the first place. Judas was a son of perdition from the beginning. His conversion was spurious. Jesus did not pray for his restoration. Judas did not lose the Holy Spirit, because he never had the Holy Spirit.

Biblical Warnings about Falling Away

Probably the strongest arguments the Arminians offer against the doctrine of the perseverance of the saints are drawn from the manifold warnings in Scripture against falling away. Paul, for example, writes: "But I discipline my body and bring it into subjection, lest, when I have preached to others, I myself should become disqualified" (1 Corinthians 9:27).

Paul elsewhere speaks of men who have been apostate: "And their message will spread like cancer. Hymenaeus and Philetus are of this sort, who have strayed concerning the truth, saying that the resurrection is already past; and they overthrow the faith of some" (2 Timothy 2:17-18).

These passages suggest that it is possible for believers to be "disqualified" or to have their faith "overthrown." It is important, however, to see how Paul concludes his statement to Timothy.

"Nevertheless the solid foundation of God stands, having this seal: 'The Lord knows those who are His,' and 'Let everyone who names the name of Christ depart from iniquity'" (v. 19).

Peter also speaks of washed pigs wallowing again and dogs who return to their vomit, comparing them to people who have turned away after being instructed in the way of righteousness. These are false converts whose natures have never been changed (see 2 Peter 2:22).

Hebrews 6

The text that contains the most solemn warning against falling away is also the most controversial regarding the doctrine of perseverance. It is found in Hebrews 6:

> For it is impossible for those who were once enlightened, and have tasted the heavenly gift, and have become partakers of the Holy Spirit, and have tasted the good word of God and the powers of the age to come, if they fall away, to renew them again to repentance, since they crucify again for themselves the Son of God, and put Him to open shame. (vv. 4-6)

This passage strongly suggests that believers can and do fall away, totally and finally. How are we to understand it?

The full meaning of the passage is difficult for several reasons. The first is that we do not know for sure what issue of apostasy was involved in this text, since we are not certain of either the author or the destination of Hebrews. There were two burning issues in the early church that easily could have provoked this dire warning.

The first issue was the problem of the so-called *lapsi*. The *lapsi* were those people who during severe persecution did not keep the faith. Not every church member went to the lions singing hymns. Some broke down and recanted their faith. Some even betrayed their comrades and collaborated with the Romans. When the persecutions died down, some of these former collaborators repented and sought readmission to the church. How they were to be received was no small controversy.

The other burning issue was that provoked by the Judaizers. The destructive influence of this group is dealt with in several parts of the New Testament, most notably in the book of Galatians. The Judaizers wanted to profess Christ and at the same time enforce the Old Testament cultic ceremonies. They insisted, for example, on ceremonial circumcision. I believe that it was the Judaizer heresy with which the author of Hebrews was concerned.

A second problem is to identify the nature of people who are being warned against falling away in Hebrews. Are they true believers or are they tares growing among the wheat? We must remember that there are three categories of people we are concerned with here. There are (1) believers, (2) unbelievers in the church, and (3) unbelievers outside of the church.

The letter to the Hebrews draws several parallels with Old Testament Israel, especially with those in the camp who were apostates. Who are these people in Hebrews? How are they described? Let us list their attributes:

1. *once enlightened*
2. *tasted the heavenly gift*
3. *partakers of the Holy Spirit*
4. *tasted the good Word of God*
5. *cannot be renewed again to repentance*

At first glance this list certainly appears to describe true believers. However it may also be describing church members who are not believers, people who have made a false profession of faith. All of these attributes may be possessed by nonbelievers. The tares who come to church every week hear the Word of God taught and preached and thus are "enlightened." They participate in all of the means of grace. They join in the Lord's Supper. They partake of the Holy Spirit in the sense that they enjoy the nearness of his special immediate presence and his benefits. They have even made a kind of repentance, at least outwardly.

Many Calvinists thereby find a solution to this passage by relating it to nonbelievers in the church who repudiate Christ. I am not entirely satisfied by that interpretation. I think this passage may well be describing true Christians. The most important phrase for me is "renew again to repentance." I know there is a false kind of repentance that the author elsewhere calls the repentance of Esau. But here he speaks of renewal. The new repentance, if it is renewed, must be like the old repentance. The renewed repentance of which he speaks is certainly the genuine kind. I assume therefore that the old was likewise genuine.

I think the author here is arguing in what we call an *ad hominem* style. An *ad hominem* argument is carried out by taking your opponent's position and carrying it to its logical conclusion. The logical conclusion of the Judaizer heresy is to destroy any hope of salvation.

The logic goes like this: If a person embraced Christ and trusted in his atonement for sin, what would that person have if he went back to the covenant of Moses? In effect he would be repudiating the finished work of Christ. He would once again be a debtor to the law. If that were the case, where would he turn for salvation? He has repudiated the cross; he couldn't turn to that. He would have no hope of salvation, because he would have no Savior. His theology does not allow a finished work of Christ.

The key to Hebrews 6 is found in verse 9. "But, beloved, we are confident of better things concerning you, yes, things that accompany salvation, though we speak in this manner."

Here the author himself notes that he is speaking in an unusual manner. His conclusion differs from those who find here a text for falling away. He concludes with a confidence of *better things* from the beloved, things that accompany salvation. Obviously falling away does not accompany salvation. The author does not say that any believer actually does fall away. In fact he says the opposite, that he is confident they will not fall away.

But if no one falls away, why even bother to warn people against it? It seems frivolous to exhort people to avoid the impossible. Here is where we must understand the relationship of perseverance to preservation. Perseverance is both a grace and a duty. We are to strive with all our might in our spiritual walk. Humanly speaking, it is possible to fall away. Yet as we strive we are to look to God who is preserving us. It is impossible that he should fail to keep us. Consider again the analogy of the child walking with his father. It is possible that the child will let go. If the father is God, it is not possible that he will let go. Even given the promise of the Father not to let go, it is still the duty of the child to hold on tightly. Thus the author of Hebrews warns believers against falling away. Luther called this the "evangelical use of exhortation." It reminds us of our duty to be diligent in our walk with God.

Finally, with respect to perseverance and preservation, we must look to the promise of God in the Old Testament. Through the prophet Jeremiah, God promises to make a new covenant with his people, a covenant that is everlasting. He says:

And I will make an everlasting covenant with them, that I will not turn away from doing them good; but I will put My fear in their hearts so that they will not depart from Me. (Jeremiah 32:40)

SUMMARY OF CHAPTER 8

1. We conclude that assurance of our salvation is vital to our spiritual lives. Without it our growth is stifled, and we are assailed with crippling doubts.
2. God calls us to make our election sure, to find the comfort and strength that God offers in assurance. In Romans 15 Paul declares that it is God who is the source or fountainhead of our perseverance and encouragement (v. 5) and of our hope (v. 13). Finding our assurance is both a duty and a privilege.
3. No true believer ever loses his salvation. To be sure, Christians fall at times seriously and radically, but never fully and finally. We persevere, not because of our strength but because of God's grace that preserves us.

For Further Study

Depart from evil, and do good; and dwell forevermore. For the LORD loves justice, and does not forsake His saints; they are preserved forever, but the descendants of the wicked shall be cut off. The righteous shall inherit the land, and dwell in it forever. (PSALM 37:27-29)

The LORD preserves all who love Him, but all the wicked He will destroy. (PSALM 145:20)

For the LORD gives wisdom; from His mouth come knowledge and understanding; He stores up sound wisdom for the upright; He is a shield to those who walk uprightly; He guards the paths of justice, and preserves the way of His saints. (PROVERBS 2:6-8)

My sheep hear My voice, and I know them, and they follow Me. And I give them eternal life, and they shall never perish; neither shall anyone snatch them out of My hand. My Father, who has given them to Me, is greater than all; and no one is able to snatch them out of My Father's hand. I and My Father are one. (JOHN 10:27-30)

For I am persuaded that neither death nor life, nor angels nor principalities nor powers, nor things present nor things to come, nor height nor depth, nor any other created thing, shall be able to separate us from the love of God which is in Christ Jesus our Lord. (ROMANS 8:38-39)

For by one offering He has perfected forever those who are being sanctified. (HEBREWS 10:14)

Now to Him who is able to keep you from stumbling, and to present you faultless before the presence of His glory with exceeding joy, to God our Savior, Who alone is wise, be glory and majesty, dominion and power, both now and forever. Amen. (JUDE 1:24-25)

CHAPTER NINE

QUESTIONS AND OBJECTIONS CONCERNING PREDESTINATION

There remain several problems and issues surrounding predestination that we must at least touch upon.

Is Predestination Fatalism?

A frequent objection raised against predestination is that it is a religious form of fatalism. If we examine fatalism in its literal sense we see that it is as far removed from the biblical doctrine of predestination as the East is from the West. Fatalism literally means that the affairs of men are controlled either by whimsical sub-deities (the Fates) or more popularly by the impersonal forces of chance.

Predestination is based neither on a mythical view of goddesses playing with our lives nor upon a view of destiny controlled by the chance collision of atoms. Predestination is rooted in the character of a personal and righteous God, a God who is the sovereign Lord of history. That my destiny would ultimately be in the hands of an indifferent or hostile force is terrifying. That it is in the hands of a righteous and loving God is quite another matter. Atoms have no righteousness in them; they are at best amoral. God is altogether holy. I prefer that my destiny be with him.

The great superstition of modern times is focused on the role given to chance in human affairs. Chance is the new reigning deity of the modern mind. Chance inhabits the castle of the gods. Chance is given credit for the creation of the universe and the emergence of the human race from the slime.

Chance is a shibboleth. It is a magic word we use to explain the unknown. It is the favorite power of causality for those who will attribute power to anything or anyone but God. This superstitious attitude toward chance is not new. We read of its attraction very early in biblical history.

We remember the incident in Jewish history when the sacred Ark of the Covenant was captured by the Philistines. On that day death visited the house of Eli and the Glory departed from Israel. The Philistines were jubilant over their victory, but they soon learned to rue the day. Wherever they took the Ark, calamity befell them. The temple of Dagon was humiliated. The people were devastated by tumors. For seven months the Ark was shuttled between the great cities of the Philistines with the same catastrophic results in each city.

In desperation the kings of the Philistines took counsel together and decided to send the Ark back to the Jews with a ransom as well, to mollify the wrath of God. Their final words of counsel are noteworthy:

> Then take the ark of the LORD and set it on the cart; and put the articles of gold which you are returning to Him as

a trespass offering in a chest by its side. Then send it away, and let it go.

And watch: if it goes up the road to its own territory, to Beth Shemesh, then He has done us this great evil. But if not, then we shall know that it is not His hand that struck us; it was by chance that it happened to us. (1 Samuel 6:8-9)

We have already noted that chance can do nothing because it is nothing. Let me elaborate. We use the word *chance* to describe mathematical possibilities. For example, when we flip a coin we say that it has a 50–50 chance to come up heads. If we call heads on the toss and it turns up tails, we might say that our luck was bad and that we missed our chance.

How much influence does chance have on the toss of a coin? What makes the coin turn up heads or tails? Would the odds change if we knew which side the coin started on, how much pressure was exerted by the thumb, how dense the atmosphere was, and how many revolutions the coin made in the air? With this knowledge, our ability to predict the outcome would far exceed 50–50.

But the hand is faster than the eye. We can't measure all these factors in the normal tossing of the coin. Since we can reduce the possible outcome to two, we simplify matters by talking about chance. The point to remember, however, is that chance exercises absolutely no influence on the coin toss. Why not? As we keep saying, chance can do nothing because it *is* nothing. It is *no thing*. Before something can exert power or influence it must first be something. It must be some kind of entity, either physical or nonphysical. Chance is neither. It is merely a mental construct. It has no power because it has no being. It is nothing.

To say that something has happened by chance is to say that it is a coincidence. This is simply a confession that we cannot perceive all the forces and causal powers that are at work in an event. Just as we cannot see all that is happening in a coin toss with the naked eye, so the complex affairs of life are also beyond our exact ability to penetrate. So we invent the term *chance* to explain them. Chance really explains nothing. It is merely a word we use as shorthand for our ignorance.

I once wrote on the subject of cause and effect, and a professor of philosophy wrote to me complaining of my naïve understanding of the law of cause and effect. He chided me for failing to take into account "uncaused events." I thanked him for his letter and said that I would be happy to grapple with his objection if he would write back and provide just one example of an uncaused event. I am still waiting. In fact, I will wait forever, because even God cannot have an uncaused event. Waiting for an uncaused event is like waiting for a square circle.

Our destinies are not controlled by chance. I say that dogmatically with all the bluster I can manage. I know that my destiny is not controlled by chance because I know that nothing can be controlled by chance. Chance can control nothing because it is nothing. What are the chances that the universe was created by chance or that our destinies are controlled by chance? Not a chance.

Fatalism finds its most popular expression in astrology. Our daily horoscopes are compiled on the basis of the movements of the stars. People in our society know more about the twelve signs of the zodiac than they do about the twelve tribes of Israel. Yet Reuben has more to do with my future than Aquarius, Judah more than Gemini.

Doesn't the Bible Say That God Is Not Willing That Any Should Perish?

The apostle Peter clearly states that God is not willing that any should perish.

> The Lord is not slack concerning His promise, as some count slackness, but is longsuffering toward us, not willing that any should perish but that all should come to repentance. (2 Peter 3:9)

How can we square this verse with predestination? If it is not the will of God to elect everyone unto salvation, how can the Bible then say that God is not willing that any should perish?

In the first place we must understand that the Bible speaks of the will of God in more than one way. For example, the Bible speaks of what we call God's *sovereign efficacious will*. The sovereign will of God is that will by which God brings things to pass with absolute certainty. Nothing can resist the will of God in this sense. By his sovereign will he created the world. The light could not have refused to shine.

The second way in which the Bible speaks of the will of God is with respect to what we call his *preceptive will*. God's preceptive will refers to his commands, his laws. It is God's will that we do the things he mandates. We are capable of disobeying this will. We do in fact break his commandments. We cannot do it with impunity. And yes, we do it without his permission or sanction. Yet we do it. We sin.

A third way the Bible speaks of the will of God has reference to God's disposition, to what is pleasing to him. God does not take delight in the death of the wicked. There is a sense in which the punishment of the wicked does not bring joy to God. He chooses to do it because it is good to punish evil. He delights in the righteousness of his judgment but is "sad" that such righteous judgment must be carried out. It is something like a judge sitting on a bench and sentencing his own son to prison.

Let us apply these three possible definitions to the passage in 2 Peter. If we take the blanket statement, "God is not willing that any should perish," and apply the sovereign efficacious will to it, the conclusion is obvious. No one will perish. If God sovereignly decrees that no one should perish, and God is God, then certainly no one will ever perish. This would then be a proof text not for Arminianism but for universalism. The text would then prove too much for Arminians.

Suppose we apply the definition of the preceptive will of God to this passage? Then the passage would mean that God does not *allow* anyone to perish. That is, he forbids the perishing of people. It is against his law. If people then went ahead and perished, God would have to punish them for perishing. His punishment for perishing would be more perishing. But how does one engage in more perishing than perishing? This definition will not work in this passage. It makes no sense.

The third alternative is that God takes no delight in the perishing of people. This squares with what the Bible says elsewhere about God's disposition toward the lost. This definition could fit this passage. Peter may simply be saying here that God takes no delight in the perishing of anyone.

Though the third definition is a possible and attractive one to use in resolving this passage with what the Bible teaches about predestination, there is yet another factor to be considered. The text says more than simply that God is not willing that any should perish. The whole clause is important: "but is longsuffering toward us, not willing that any should perish but that all should come to repentance."

What is the antecedent of *any*? It is clearly *us*. Does *us* refer to all of us humans? Or does it refer to us Christians, the people of God? Peter is fond of speaking of the elect as a special group of people. I think what he is saying here is that God does not will that any of us (the elect) perish. If that is his meaning, then the text would demand the first definition and would be one more strong passage in favor of predestination.

In two different ways the text may easily be harmonized with predestination. In no way does it support Arminianism. Its only other possible meaning would be universalism, which would then bring it into conflict with everything else the Bible says against universalism.

If I Can Only Choose What God Has Already Decreed, Then How Can My Choice Be a Real Choice?

I sometimes hear non-Calvinist thinkers (whom we will refer to collectively as Arminians) object to the Calvinist understanding of free will, believing that God's ordination of whatsoever comes to pass renders the concept of "choice" meaningless. There is no point, they say, to looking at Jonathan Edwards's talk about the reasons for our choices since God foreordains our decisions and makes us unable to do other than that which he has ordained. This is a significant objection, but it does not refute Calvinism. Let us look at the unspoken assumptions that lay behind this question and we will see its weaknesses.

First, Arminians assume that human choices based on God's eternal decrees cannot be "real" because the decrees set these decisions in stone. Human beings cannot choose otherwise if the Lord has decreed what will happen, and without the ability to choose otherwise, we do not have free will in any meaningful sense. At the same time, most of our Arminian friends affirm God's full knowledge of the future and say the reality of human choice remains despite his exhaustive foreknowledge. The assumption seems to be that God's knowledge of our future decisions is consistent with "real" choices because his mere knowledge of what will occur does not establish the future. God, in eternity past, is just a passive observer of human choices, making people the final determining agents in their decision-making.

Yet the Arminian view of human decision-making does not actually preserve the "reality" of human choices in the way Arminians define "real" choices. If God is meaningfully omniscient, as most Arminians believe, then his knowledge of the future renders it impossible that our decisions could ever be other than what he already knows they will be. God's knowledge cannot be increased or diminished, so he will not learn something new tomorrow that will change my future decision for or against Christ. I do not have the "real choice," as Arminians define it, to say yes or no to Jesus if God knows certainly today that I will say yes tomorrow. The only way to maintain the Arminian definition of "real" choice would be to deny that God's omniscience makes the future certain; we would have to deny that God has full knowledge of all future events. Some have gone this route, but most Arminians refuse to take the step needed to preserve the "reality of choice" and deny God's knowledge of the future. To deny this knowledge to God is so plainly unbiblical that the vast majority of Arminians have never thought of such heresy. Ultimately, most Arminians are inconsistently biblical, affirming the biblical teaching that God knows the future while at the same time denying the biblical positions that God is sovereign even over our choices and that his omniscience invalidates their view of free will. Still, to be *inconsistently biblical* is far better than it is to be *consistently unbiblical* and deny the biblical truths that God knows the future and that he is sovereign over all things, even the human will.

The second faulty assumption behind the question at hand is that choices are only "real" if God has not ordained them. Yet Scripture never says the reality of our choices depends on the Lord not ordaining whatsoever comes to pass. The Bible, we have seen, affirms the reality of human choices in the same events where it affirms God's work of predestination (see Genesis 50:15-21; Acts 2:22-24). True, we cannot understand fully how these truths fit together, but our lack of understanding does not mean the reality of our choices and divine predestination are therefore incompatible. All this lack of understanding reveals is the deficiency of our knowledge and the degree to which sin impacts our ability to think God's thoughts after him (see Romans 1:18-32).

An important concept that is related to the classical doctrine of the providence of God is the notion of concurrence. Concurrence or confluence refers to the way in which human decisions are made under the sovereign will of God's divine decisions without destroying the reality or responsibility of the human decisions. A classic example of this is found in Genesis 50 when Joseph's brothers feared retaliation from his hand. He replied to them in verse 19 by saying, "Do not be afraid, for am I in the place of God, but as for you, you meant evil against me; but God meant it for good, in order to bring it about as it is this day to save many people alive." Here we see a distinction between God's intent and the intent of Joseph's wicked brothers. Joseph's brothers acted volitionally, that is they acted with real intentionality. God was working at the same time with his intentionality. He brought to pass his purpose through the sinful choices of Joseph's brothers. The same principle is at work with respect to the death of Christ. Christ is delivered into the hands of the wicked according to the counsel of God. It was the will of God that Jesus suffer and die at the hands of wicked men. Their choices to crucify him were real choices, and choices for which they were altogether culpable. They meant it for evil, but God meant it for good.

Let me make one final point. Jonathan Edwards's discussion of free will is vital because it accounts for how our human experience confirms the reality of our choices. We "feel" that we make real choices, and while our experience cannot be the final norm for our theology, neither can we deny its importance. We believe and feel that our choices are real because we have real wills with real inclinations, preferences, and so forth even as all that we decide is part of God's sovereign will. Edwards's analysis helps us better understand how our experience of human choice and the decrees of the Lord fit together in a way that preserves human responsibility and divine sovereignty without these two elements devolving into a logical contradiction.

If God Actively Ordains "Whatsoever Comes to Pass," How Can Calvinists Speak of God Acting Passively to "Allow" or "Permit" Evil?

You rightly notice an apparent difficulty with Calvinists speaking of God permitting some things even as we also speak of his ordaining "whatsoever comes to pass." It is a distinction that Reformed thinkers have often used even though we have always been careful to clarify what we mean by "permission." John Calvin deals with the question at length in his commentary on Genesis 45, and I commend that discussion to you for further study.

Theologians must always choose the words that will best convey the biblical truth they want to summarize and proclaim. Entire doctrinal controversies have been settled through the removal or addition of just one letter to a theological term, so you can imagine the intricacies of distinguishing between God actively ordaining good things in contrast to his more passively permitting evil. Basically, we speak of God "permitting" evil in order to show that in his eternal decrees, God's relationship to evil is not the same as his relationship to what is good. The way he stands behind evil events in his providence is more indirect than the way he stands behind good events. The terms *permit* or *allow* represent our attempt to put into words that which is far beyond our comprehension, namely, that God ordains evil without ever being culpable for that evil himself (see James 1:13, 16; 1 John 1:5). Calvin notes in his commentary on Genesis 45:8 that "this method of acting is secret, and far above our understanding," and I suspect that it might remain so even into eternity. In any case, God is certainly never just a passive observer of what happens; nevertheless, he brings all things to pass without ever being responsible for evil even as he is always to be praised for the good that occurs.

It is important to remember that when we speak of God's permitting evil to exist that this permission is not a contradiction of his active ordination. What God ordains passively, he actively chooses to ordain. The difference here between active and passive is the difference between God's doing evil and ordaining that evil come to pass. We are told in the Bible that we are never to call evil good, or good evil. It's one thing to say that evil is good. It is quite another to say that it is good that there is evil. If it is not good that there is evil, then God's ordaining that evil should come to pass would itself be an evil act on the part of God. But what if God, to manifest his own glory, sovereignly decreed that evil should come to pass, that he might make known the riches of his glory and of his mercy. Then that ordaining of the entrance of evil into the world is a good decision on God's part. If God does not have the ability sovereignly to bring good out of evil, then one of the most comforting texts that we have in sacred Scripture would be immediately lost to us. Romans 8:28 teaches that all things work together for good for those who love the Lord and who are the called according to his purpose. This does not mean that all things considered in and of themselves are good things, but rather that God can and does redeem evil things by working them together for good. This makes God sovereign over evil but not guilty for his sovereign ordination.

Since God Intervenes in the Hearts of the Elect to Ensure Their Salvation but Passes by Others without Creating Unbelief in Their Hearts, How Did People Fall into Unbelief in the First Place? Was Humanity's Choice to Sin Not Part of God's Decree?

This question gets right to the heart of the problem of evil, which asks this question: How can evil exist if the Creator is perfectly good, omniscient, and omnipotent? The greatest minds in history have applied themselves to this question, but there is as yet not one answer that "solves" the problem in a way that eliminates every question or difficulty. We are faced here with a great mystery God has not chosen to reveal in its entirety, at least not yet.

Is there nothing then that can be said? Of course not. Again, we turn to Scripture as our only infallible authority to see what has been revealed about evil. First, we know that God is entirely sovereign over everything that ever happens. He "works all things according to the counsel of His will" (Ephesians 1:11), so nothing occurs apart from his sovereign decrees. There is no doubt that "all things" includes evil, even the choice of Adam to sin in the first place and plunge creation into a state of misery and decay (see Job 1:20-22; Proverbs 16:4; Isaiah 45:7; Lamentations 3:38; Mark 14:17-21). Secondly, Scripture is clear that God can ordain evil without ever being responsible or culpable for it. He "cannot be tempted by evil, nor does He himself tempt anyone" (James 1:13), and he is the holy Creator who is free from every stain (see Isaiah 6:1–3).

Perhaps we will one day know how these truths fit together fully, but right now all I can confess is that I do not know how humanity fell into unbelief. I know that God ordained the Fall, but I do not know how this ordination enabled Adam and his descendants to fall into sin without the Lord himself being the direct, culpable agent for the Fall. However the Fall came about, blame for Adam's sin cannot be laid at the Lord's feet in any way. Because God ordained that evil should exist, I know that in some sense it is good that evil exists. I am not saying that evil *is good* but only that God *deemed it good* to allow evil to infect his creation so that he could overcome wickedness to the praise of his glory. Scripture does not allow us to say any more than this, and if the Word of God is our authority, then here is where we must stop and be silent, trusting in the goodness of God who in his wisdom has ordained all things, even that which is sad and tragic.

What Is the Unpardonable Sin?

In our discussions on assurance of salvation and the perseverance of the saints, we touched on the question of the unforgivable sin.

The fact that Jesus warns against the committing of a sin that is unforgivable is beyond dispute. The questions we must face, then, are these: What is the unforgivable sin? Can Christians commit this sin?

Jesus defined it as blasphemy against the Holy Spirit:

> Therefore I say to you, every sin and blasphemy will be forgiven men, but the blasphemy against the Spirit will not be forgiven men.
>
> Anyone who speaks a word against the Son of Man, it will be forgiven him; but whoever speaks against the Holy Spirit, it will not be forgiven him, either in this age or in the age to come. (Matthew 12:31-32)

In this text Jesus does not provide a detailed explanation of the nature of this dreadful sin. He declares that there is such a sin and gives an ominous warning about it. The rest of the New Testament adds little in the way of further explanation. As a result of this silence, there has been much speculation about the unforgivable sin.

Two sins have been frequently mentioned as candidates for the unforgivable sin: adultery and murder. Adultery is chosen on the grounds that it represents a sin against the Holy Spirit because the body is the temple of the Holy Spirit. Adultery was a capital crime in the Old Testament. The reasoning is that, since it deserved the death penalty and involved a violation of the temple of the Holy Spirit, this must be the unpardonable sin.

Murder is chosen for similar reasons. Since man is created in the image of God, an attack upon the human person is considered an attack upon God himself. To slay the image-bearer is to insult the One whose image is borne. Likewise murder is a capital sin.

We add to this the fact that murder is a sin against the sanctity of life. Since the Holy Spirit is the ultimate "life force," to kill a human being is to insult the Holy Spirit.

As attractive as these theories may be to speculators, they have not gained the consent of most biblical scholars. A more popular view has to do with the final resistance to the Holy Spirit's application of Christ's work of redemption. Final unbelief is then seen as the unpardonable sin. If a person repeatedly, fully, and finally repudiates the gospel, then there is no hope of future forgiveness.

What all three of these theories lack is a serious consideration of the meaning of blasphemy. Blasphemy is something that we do with our mouths. It deals with what we say out loud. Certainly it can also be done with the pen, but blasphemy is a *verbal* sin.

The Ten Commandments include a prohibition against blasphemy. We are forbidden to make frivolous or irreverent use of the name of God. In God's eyes the verbal abuse of his holy name is a serious enough matter to make it to his top ten list of commands. This tells us that blasphemy is a serious matter in God's sight. It is a heinous sin to blaspheme any member of the Godhead.

Does this mean that anyone who has ever abused the name of God has no possible hope of forgiveness, now or ever? Does it mean that if a person curses once, using the name of God, that he is doomed forever? I think not.

It is crucial to note in this text that Jesus makes a distinction between sinning against him (the Son of Man), and sinning against the Holy Spirit. Does this mean that it is okay to blaspheme the first person of the Trinity and the second person of the Trinity, but to insult the third person is to cross the boundaries of forgiveness? This hardly makes sense.

Why, then, would Jesus make such a distinction between sinning against himself and against the Holy Spirit? I think the key to answering this question is the key to the whole question of the blasphemy against the Holy Spirit. That key is found in the context in which Jesus originally gave his severe warning.

In Matthew 12:24 we read: "But when the Pharisees heard it they said, 'This fellow does not cast out demons except by Beelzebub, the ruler of the demons.'" Jesus responds with a discourse about a house divided against itself and the foolishness of the idea that Satan would work to cast out Satan. His warning about the unpardonable sin is the conclusion of this discussion. He introduces his severe warning with the word *therefore*.

The situation runs something like this: The Pharisees are being repeatedly critical of Jesus. Their verbal attacks upon him get more and more vicious. Jesus had been casting out demons "by the finger of God," which means by the Holy Spirit. The Pharisees sink so low as to accuse Jesus of doing his holy work by the power of Satan. Jesus warns them. It is as if he were saying: "Be careful. Be really careful. You are coming perilously close to a sin for which you cannot be forgiven. It is one thing to attack me, but watch yourselves. You're treading on holy ground here."

We still wonder why Jesus made the distinction between sinning against the Son of Man and sinning against the Spirit. We notice that even from the cross Jesus pled for the forgiveness of those who were murdering him. On the day of Pentecost Peter spoke of the horrible crime against Christ committed in the Crucifixion, yet still held out hope for forgiveness to those who had participated in it. Paul says, "But we speak the wisdom of God in a mystery, the hidden wisdom which God ordained before the ages for our glory, *which none of the rulers of this age knew; for had they known, they would not have crucified the Lord of glory*" (1 Corinthians 2:7-8, emphasis added).

These texts indicate an allowance of sorts for human ignorance.

We must remember that when the Pharisees accused Jesus of working by the power of Satan they did not yet have the benefit of the fullness of God's disclosure of the true identity of Christ. These charges were made *before* the Resurrection. To be sure, the Pharisees *should* have recognized Christ, but they did not. Jesus' words from the cross are important: "Father, forgive them, for they *know not* what they do."

When Jesus gave the warning and distinguished between blasphemy against the Son of Man and blasphemy against the Holy Spirit it was at a time when he had not yet been made fully manifest. We note that this distinction tends to fall away after the Resurrection, Pentecost, and the Ascension. Note what the author of Hebrews declares:

> For if we sin willfully after we have received the knowledge of the truth, there no longer remains a sacrifice for sins, but a certain fearful expectation of judgment, and fiery indignation which will devour the adversaries. Anyone who has rejected Moses' law dies without mercy on the testimony of two or three witnesses. Of how much worse punishment, do you suppose, will he be thought worthy who has trampled the Son of God underfoot, counted the blood of the covenant by which he was sanctified a common thing, and insulted the Spirit of grace? (Hebrews 10:26-29)

In this passage the distinction between sinning against Christ and against the Spirit falls away. Here, to sin against Christ is to insult the Spirit of grace. The key is in the willful sin *after* we have received the knowledge of the truth.

If we take the first line of this text as an absolute, none of us has a hope of heaven. We all sin willfully after we know the truth. A specific sin is in view here, not each and every sin. I am persuaded that the specific sin in view here is blasphemy against the Holy Spirit.

I agree with the New Testament scholars who conclude that the unforgivable sin is to blaspheme Christ *and* the Holy Spirit by saying Jesus is a devil when you know better. That is, the unforgivable sin cannot be done in ignorance. If a person knows with certainty that Jesus is the Son of God and then declares with his mouth that Jesus is of Satan, that person has committed unpardonable blasphemy.

Who commits such a sin? This is a sin common to devils and to totally degenerate people. Satan knew who Jesus was. He could not plead ignorance as an excuse.

One of the fascinating facts of history is the strange way in which unbelievers speak of Jesus. The vast majority of unbelievers speak of Jesus with great respect. They may attack the church with great hostility but still speak of Jesus as a "great man." Only once in my life have I heard a person say out loud that Jesus was a devil. I was shocked to see a man stand in the middle of the street shaking his fist toward heaven and screaming at the top of his lungs. He cursed God and used every obscenity he could utter in attacking Jesus. I was equally shocked only hours later when I saw the same man on a stretcher with a bullet hole in his chest. It was self-inflicted. He died before morning.

Even that dreadful sight did not drive me to the conclusion that the man had actually committed the unpardonable sin. I had no way of knowing if he was ignorant of Christ's true identity or not.

Saying that Jesus is a devil is not something we see many people do. It is, however, possible for people to know the truth of Jesus and sink this low. One does not need to be born again to have an intellectual knowledge of the true identity of Jesus. Again, the unregenerate demons know who he is.

What of Christians? Is it possible for a Christian to commit the unforgivable sin and thereby lose his salvation? I think not. The grace of God makes it impossible. In ourselves we are capable of any sin, including blasphemy against the Holy Spirit. But God preserves us from this sin. He preserves us from full and final blasphemy, guarding our lips from this horrible crime. We perform other sins and other kinds of blasphemy, but God in his grace restrains us from committing the ultimate blasphemy.

Did Jesus Die for Everyone?

One of the most controversial points of Reformed theology concerns the *L* in TULIP. *L* stands for *Limited Atonement*. It has been such a problem of doctrine that there are multitudes of Christians who say they embrace most of the doctrines of Calvinism but get off the boat here. They refer to themselves as "four-point" Calvinists. The point they cannot abide is limited atonement.

I have often thought that to be a four-point Calvinist one must misunderstand at least one of the five points. It is hard for me to imagine that anyone could understand the other four points of Calvinism and deny limited atonement. There always is the possibility, however, of the happy inconsistency by which people hold incompatible views at the same time.

The doctrine of limited atonement is so complex that to treat it adequately demands a full volume. I have not even given it a full chapter in this book because a chapter cannot do it justice. I have thought about not mentioning it altogether because the danger exists that to say too little about it is worse than saying nothing at all. But I think the reader deserves at least a brief summary of the doctrine as it pertains to predestination. So I will proceed—with the caution that the subject requires a much deeper treatment than I am able to provide here.

The issue of limited atonement concerns the question, "For whom did Christ die? Did he die for everybody or only for the elect?" We all agree that the value of Jesus' atonement was great enough to cover the sins of every human being. We also agree that his atonement is truly offered to all men. Any person who places his trust in the atoning death of Jesus Christ will most certainly receive the full benefits of that atonement. We are also confident that anyone who responds to the universal offer of the gospel will be saved.

The question is, "For whom was the atonement *designed*?" Did God send Jesus into the world merely to make salvation *possible* for people? Or did God have something more definite in mind? (Roger Nicole, the eminent Baptist theologian, prefers to call limited atonement "Definite Atonement," disrupting the acrostic TULIP as much as I do.)

Some argue that all limited atonement means is that the benefits of the atonement are limited to believers who meet the necessary condition of faith. That is, though Christ's atonement was sufficient to cover the sins of all men and to satisfy God's justice against all sin, it only *effects* salvation for believers. The formula reads: Sufficient for all; efficient for the elect only.

That point simply serves to distinguish us from universalists who believe that the atonement secured salvation for everyone. But the doctrine of limited atonement goes further than that. It is concerned with the deeper question of the Father's and the Son's *intention* in the Cross. It declares that the mission and death of Christ was restricted to a limited number—to his people, his sheep. Jesus was named *Jesus* because he would save his people from their sins (see Matthew 1:21). The Good Shepherd lays down his life for the sheep (see John 10:15). Such passages are found liberally in the New Testament.

The mission of Christ was to save the elect. "This is the will of the Father who sent Me, that of all He has given Me I should lose nothing, but should raise it up at the last day" (John 6:39). Had there not been a fixed number contemplated by God when he appointed Christ to die, then the effects of Christ's death would have been uncertain. It would be possible that the mission of Christ would have been a dismal and complete failure.

Jesus' atonement and his intercession are joint works of his high priesthood. He explicitly excludes the non-elect from his great High Priestly Prayer: "I do not pray for the world but for those whom you have given Me" (John 17:9). Did Christ die for those for whom he would not pray?

The essential issue here concerns the nature of the Atonement. Jesus' atonement included both *expiation* and *propitiation*. Expiation involves Christ's removing our sins "away from" (*ex*) us. Pro-pitiation involves a satisfaction of sin "before or in the presence of" (*pro*) God. Arminianism has an atonement that is limited in value. It does not cover the sin of unbelief. If Jesus died for all the sins of all men, if he expiated all our sins and propitiated all our sins, then everybody would be saved. A potential atonement is not a real atonement. Jesus *really* atoned for the sins of his sheep.

The biggest problem with definite or limited atonement is found in the passages that the Scriptures use concerning Christ's death "for all" or for the "whole world." The world for whom Christ died cannot mean the entire human family. It must refer to the universality of the elect (people from every tribe and nation) or to the inclusion of Gentiles in addition to the world of the Jews. It was a Jew who wrote that Jesus did not die merely for *our* sins but for the sins of the whole world. Does the word *our* refer to believers or to believing Jews?

We must remember that one of the cardinal points of the New Testament concerned the inclusion of the Gentiles in God's plan of salvation. Salvation was *of* the Jews but not restricted to the Jews. Wherever it is said that Christ died for all, some limitation must be added or the conclusion would have to be universalism or a mere potential atonement.

Christ's atonement was real. It effected all that God and Jesus intended by it. The design of God was not and cannot be frustrated by human unbelief. The sovereign God sovereignly sent his Son to atone for his people.

Our election is in Christ. We are saved by him, in him, and *for* him. The motive for our salvation is not merely the love God has for us. It is especially grounded in the love the Father has for the Son. God insists that his Son will see the travail of his soul and be satisfied. There never has been the slightest possibility that Christ could have died in vain. If man is truly dead in sin and in bondage to sin, a mere potential or conditional atonement not only *may have* ended in failure but most certainly *would have* ended in failure. Arminians have no sound reason to believe that Jesus did not die in vain. They are left with a Christ who tried to save everybody but actually saved nobody.

What Does Predestination Do to the Task of Evangelism?

This question raises grave concerns about the mission of the church. It is particularly weighty for evangelical Christians. If personal salvation is decided in advance by an immutable divine decree, what is the sense or urgency of the work of evangelism?

I will never forget the terrifying experience of being quizzed on this point by Dr. Gerstner in a seminary class. There were about twenty of us seated in a semicircle in the classroom. He posed the question: "All right, gentlemen, if God has sovereignly decreed election and reprobation from all eternity, why should we be concerned about evangelism?" I breathed a sigh of relief when Gerstner started his interrogation on the left end of the semicircle since I was sitting in the last seat on the right. I took comfort in the hope that the question would never get around to me.

The comfort was short-lived. The first student replied to Gerstner's query, "I don't know, sir. That question has always plagued me." The second student said, "It beats me." The third just shook his head and dropped his gaze toward the floor. In rapid succession the students all passed on the question. The dominoes were falling in my direction.

"Well, Mr. Sproul, how would you answer?" I wanted to vanish into thin air or find a hiding place in the floorboards, but there was no escape. I stammered and muttered a reply. Dr. Gerstner said, "Speak up!" In tentative words I said, "Well, Dr. Gerstner, I know this isn't the answer you are looking for, but one small reason we should still be concerned about evangelism is that, well, uh, you know, after all, Christ does command us to do evangelism."

Gerstner's eyes started to flame. He said, "Ah, I see, Mr. Sproul, one *small* reason is that your Savior, the Lord of Glory, the King of kings has so commanded it. A small reason, Mr. Sproul? It is barely significant to you that the same sovereign God who sovereignly decrees your election also sovereignly commands your involvement in the task of evangelism?" Oh, how I wished I'd never used the word *small*. I got Gerstner's point.

Evangelism is our duty. God has commanded it. That should be enough to end the matter. But there is more. Evangelism is not only a duty; it is also a privilege. God allows us to participate in the greatest work in human history, the work of redemption. Hear what Paul says about it. He adds a chapter 10 to his famous chapter 9 of Romans:

> For "whoever calls upon the name of the Lord shall be saved." How then shall they call on Him in whom they have not believed? And how shall they believe in Him of whom they have not heard? And how shall they hear without a preacher? And how shall they preach unless they are sent? As it is written: "How beautiful are the feet of those who preach the gospel of peace, who bring glad tidings of good things!" (Romans 10:13-15)

We notice the logic of Paul's progression here. He lists a series of necessary conditions for people to be saved. Without sending there are no preachers. Without preachers there is no preaching. Without preaching there is no hearing of the gospel. Without the hearing of the gospel there is no believing of the gospel. Without the believing of the gospel there is no calling upon God to be saved. Without the calling upon God to be saved there is no salvation.

God not only foreordains the *end* of salvation for the elect, he also foreordained the *means* to that end. God has chosen the foolishness of preaching as the means to accomplish redemption. I suppose he could have worked out his divine purpose without us. He could publish the gospel in the clouds using his holy finger in skywriting. He could preach the gospel himself, in his own voice, shouting it from heaven. But that is not his choice.

It is a marvelous privilege to be used by God in the plan of redemption. Paul appeals to an Old Testament passage when he speaks of the beauty of the feet of those who bring good tidings and publish peace.

> How beautiful upon the mountains are the feet of him
> who brings good news, who proclaims peace, who brings
> glad tiding of good things, who proclaims salvation, who
> says to Zion, "Your God reigns!" Your watchmen shall lift
> up their voices, with their voices they shall sing together;
> for they shall see eye to eye when the LORD brings
> back Zion.
> Break forth into joy, sing together, you waste places of
> Jerusalem! For the LORD has comforted His people, He has
> redeemed Jerusalem. (Isaiah 52:7-9)

In the ancient world, news of battles and other crucial events was carried by runners. The modern marathon race is named after the Battle of Marathon because of the endurance of the messenger who carried the news of the outcome home to his people.

Lookouts were posted to watch for the approaching messengers. Their eyes were sharp and trained to the subtle nuances of the strides of the approaching runners. Those bearing bad news approached with heavy feet. Those runners bearing good news approached swiftly, with feet sprinting through the dust. Their strides revealed their excitement. For the watchmen the sight of a runner approaching rapidly in the distance with his feet skimming over the mountain was a gorgeous vision to behold.

So the Bible speaks of the beauty of the feet of those who bring us good news. When my daughter was born and the doctor came to the waiting room to announce it, I wanted to hug him. We are favorably inclined to those who bring us good tidings. I will always have a special place in my affections for the man who first told me of Christ. I know that it was God who saved me and not that man, but I still appreciate the man's role in my salvation.

To lead people to Christ is one of the greatest personal blessings that we ever enjoy. To be a Calvinist takes no joy away from that experience. Historically, Calvinists have been strongly active in evangelism and world mission. We need only point to John Calvin's missionary endeavors in Geneva or to Jonathan Edwards and George Whitefield and the Great Awakening to illustrate this point.

We have a meaningful role to play in evangelism. We preach and we proclaim the gospel. That is our duty and our privilege. But it is God who brings the increase. He does not need us to accomplish his purpose, but he is pleased to use us in the task (see 1 Corinthians 3:6-7).

I once met a traveling evangelist who said to me, "Give me any man alone for fifteen minutes and I will get a decision for Christ." Sadly, the man really believed his own words. He was convinced that the power of conversion rested solely in his powers of persuasion.

I don't doubt that the man was basing his claim on his past track record. He was so overbearing that I am sure there were multitudes who made decisions for Christ within fifteen minutes of being alone with him. Sure, he could make good his promise to produce a *decision* in fifteen minutes. What he couldn't guarantee was a *conversion* in fifteen minutes. People would make decisions just to get away from him.

We must never underestimate the importance of our role in

evangelism. Neither must we overestimate it. We preach. We bear witness. We provide the outward call. But God alone has the power to call a person to himself inwardly. I do not feel cheated by that. On the contrary, I feel comforted. We must do our job, trusting that God will do his.

Conclusion

At the beginning of this book I related a bit of my own personal pilgrimage concerning the doctrine of predestination. I mentioned the earnest and long-term struggle it involved. I mentioned that I was finally brought into submission to the doctrine reluctantly. I was first brought to a conviction of the truth of the matter before I took any delight in it.

Let me close this book by mentioning that soon after I awoke to the truth of predestination I began to see the beauty of it and taste its sweetness. I have grown to love this doctrine. It is most comforting. It underlines the extent to which God has gone in our behalf. It is a theology that begins and ends with grace. It begins and ends with doxology. We praise a God who lifted us from spiritual deadness and makes us walk in high places. We find a God who is "for us," giving us the courage to withstand those who may be against us. It makes our souls rejoice to know that all things are working together for our good. We delight in our Savior who truly saves us and preserves us and intercedes for us. We marvel at his craftsmanship and in what he has wrought. We skip and kick our heels when we discover his promise to finish in us what he has started in us. We ponder mysteries and bow before them, but not without doxology for the riches of grace he has revealed:

Oh, the depth of the riches both of the wisdom and knowledge of God! . . . For of Him and through Him and to Him are all things, to whom be glory forever. Amen. (Romans 11:33, 36)

About the Author

Dr. R. C. Sproul is the founder and chairman of Ligonier Ministries, an international teaching ministry based in Lake Mary, Florida. His teaching can be heard around the United States and overseas on the daily *Renewing Your Mind* radio program. He also serves as senior minister of preaching and teaching at Saint Andrews in Sanford, Florida, and as chancellor of the Ligonier Academy of Biblical and Theological Studies.

During his distinguished academic career, Dr. Sproul has helped train men for the ministry as a professor at several theological seminaries.

He is the author of more than seventy books, including *The Holiness of God, Chosen by God, The Invisible Hand, Faith Alone, A Taste of Heaven, Truths We Confess, The Truth of the Cross,* and *What Is Reformed Theology?* He also served as general editor of *The Reformation Study Bible* and has written several children's books, including his most recent, *The Prince's Poison Cup.*

Dr. Sproul and his wife, Vesta, make their home in Longwood, Florida.

Look for these other best-selling classics from R. C. Sproul.

The Holiness of God
R. C. Sproul's best-selling treatment of an often misunderstood dimension of God's character. A must-read for anyone serious about growing in his or her faith.

Chosen by God
A clear, biblical presentation of the doctrine of predestination.

Essential Truths of the Christian Faith
Categorized for easy reference, this book gives a clear overview of more than 100 biblical doctrines that provide a basic understanding of Christianity.

Now, That's a Good Question!
A collection of more than 300 questions and answers on the Christian faith and lifestyle.